Cultural Dimensions of Well-Being

Anthropology of Well-Being
Individual, Community, Society

Series Editor

Ben G. Blount, PhD (SocioEcological Informatics)

Mission Statement

Well-being is central and important in people's daily lives and life history. This book series brings about understanding of what the complex concepts of well-being include. The concepts of quality of life, life satisfaction, and happiness will be explored and viewed at the individual level, the community level, and the level of society. The series encourages and promotes research into the concept of well-being, how it appears to be defined culturally, and how it is utilized across levels and across different social, economic, and ethnic groups. Understandings of how well-being promotes stability and resilience will also be critical to advances in understanding, as well as how well-being can be implemented as a goal in resisting vulnerabilities and in adaptation. Series books include monographs and edited collections by a range of academics, from rising scholars to experts in relevant fields.

Advisory Board Members

Steven Jacob, Kathleen Galvin, Carlos Garcia-Quijano,
Cynthia Isenhour, and Richard Pollnac

Books in Series

Intimate Partner Violence and Advocate Response: Redefining Love in Western Belize, by Melissa Beske

Contemporary Conversations on Immigration in the United States: The View from Prince George's County, Maryland, by Judith Noemí Freidenberg

Cultural Dimensions of Well-Being: Therapy Animals as Healers, by Clementine K. Fujimura and Simone Nommensen

Cultural Dimensions of Well-Being

Therapy Animals as Healers

Clementine K. Fujimura
and Simone Nommensen

LEXINGTON BOOKS
Lanham • Boulder • New York • London

Published by Lexington Books
An imprint of The Rowman & Littlefield Publishing Group, Inc.
4501 Forbes Boulevard, Suite 200, Lanham, Maryland 20706
www.rowman.com

Unit A, Whitacre Mews, 26-34 Stannary Street, London SE11 4AB

British Library Cataloguing in Publication Information Available

Library of Congress Cataloging-in-Publication Data

Names: Nommensen, Simone, 1973- author. | Fujimura, Clementine K., 1965- author.
Title: Cultural dimensions of well-being : therapy animals as healers / Simone Nommensen and
    Clementine K. Fujimura.
Description: Lanham : Lexington Books, [2018] | Series: Anthropology of well-being: individual,
    community and society | Includes bibliographical references and index.
Identifiers: LCCN 2017037219 (print) | LCCN 2017043164 (ebook)
Subjects: LCSH: Well-being. | Service dogs. | Animals--Therapeutic use. | Human-animal relation-
    ships.
Classification: LCC BF575.H27 (ebook) | LCC BF575.H27 N66 2018 (print) | DDC 615.8/5158--
    dc23
LC record available at https://lccn.loc.gov/2017037219

ISBN 9781498541275 (cloth : alk. paper)
ISBN 9781498541299 (pbk. : alk. paper)
ISBN 9781498541282 (electronic)

Printed in the United States of America

To: Bosse, Hanna, Lasse, Merle, Tristan, and Willem

Contents

Acknowledgments

It is a rare occurrence in life when profession and passion intersect. We feel grateful to all the beings in our lives, both human and canine, who made this possible for us. While each of us pursued degrees in fields dear to us, it was not until a serendipitous meeting that we discovered our overlapping interests and aspirations to combine our interest in companion animals, search and rescue, and therapy animals with our knowledge of veterinary science and cultural studies. It seemed indulgent at the time to combine our careers and pastimes into a full-fledged research project, but as we discussed our ideas with those in and outside our fields, it became clear that others were equally interested. With our families', colleagues', and friends' encouragement, we felt compelled to pursue our dream project.

First and foremost, we would like to thank our partners in life, our husbands, Paul Fujimura and Joerg Nommensen, both of whom encouraged and supported our vocations and ultimately, our working together. Without their support, it would have been impossible. Besides standing by us, they read and reread numerous iterations of chapters, diligently editing and commenting, pushing us to move forward.

Next we must thank our children for their patience and understanding, as dinners were at times less interesting, homes less tidied, and they themselves were asked to engage in numerous conversations on the subject of this book.

Friends became involved as they too discovered articles and reports important to our subject matter. Thank you, Catherine O'Neil, for your discovering Anthrozoology and supplying us with videos and articles. And to Joe Gwara, who pointed us to research involving animals, communication, and therapy outside our fields. Special thanks to Daniela E. Hahn, who was always available to discuss facts and ideas about therapy dogs and their deep impact in modern therapy. We are especially grateful to all the people that allowed us to use their personal stories in this book. Last but not least, we want to thank Walter Hügle, who supported and encouraged us during the whole process of research and writing. Thank you for your corrections and ideas whenever we lost our focus and for helping to bring us back on track.

We are, of course, also thankful to our canine companions, who endured more training than is normal for your average family dogs, as they became certified in search and rescue, tracking, and therapy, and to allow us to participate and even work in contexts where such training is needed, ultimately giving us the opportunity to gain firsthand experience in a variety of cultural and co-cultural contexts. We are hopeful that their training made them happy and also helped people and animals in need of their services, including lost pets and their owners, senior citizens as well as clients and staff in hospices. Finally, we are thankful to those we serve for allowing us to do so.

Introduction

It is late in the afternoon and Louie, a therapy dog, and I have nearly completed our visits with patients at the local hospice. We are tired, but there is one more patient we must see. We have been told he does not have long, but that he loves dogs and was the proud owner of a few himself. After knocking and hearing a weak voice beckon us in, we enter a large room with tubes and wires across the floor leading to a hospital bed. My first concern is to navigate Louie over the tubes so as not to cause a disaster. As we walk around to the bed, a thin, frail, skeletal-like figure reaches out to greet the visiting dog. Louie puts his muzzle on the bed and the gentleman responds with a weak hint of a smile and a sigh. He closes his eyes and feels Louie's head, nose, ears . . . I try to speak to the gentleman, but realize soon enough that he is too weak to respond. Instead we enjoy the silence and feeling of relaxation that seems to spread through the room. After some time, the gentleman appears to have gone to sleep and Louie and I begin our quiet exit. We do not get very far when I hear him say in no uncertain terms: "Come back. I want him to give me a high five." Louie does not give high fives. He has never done so and I cringe at the thought of letting the gentleman down. I try to explain that we are happy to stay longer, but that Louie doesn't give high fives. "Sure he does! Come here. I'll show you." I begrudgingly go back with Louie. The patient reaches out with his hand at an angle. Louie uses the step by the bed, peers over the patient's blanket and reaches to give the man his paw. Not a complete high five but high enough to make the man relax his arm and neck and smile. "See" he says, "I knew he would." I am in disbelief. I peer down at my dog who is calm but wagging his tail ever so slightly as if to confirm his success. To this day I wonder, how did Louie know what to do? I am so proud of him. I realize we have made someone very happy in a critical moment of his life.

WHY ANIMALS AND WELL-BEING?

In recent years there has been an explosion of literature attesting to the respectable and at times extraordinary benefits of companion animals and uses of non-human animals for improving human well-being. Given our cohabitation with such animals (which from now on will mostly be referred to as "animals") for the past centuries, how is it that only recently do we begin to associate animals with benefits to our health? Why is it that some societies do not value animals as therapists the way others do? And to what extent is it fair to the animals that humans use them as such? This book discusses ways in which we relate to our animals including for comfort, healing, and in developing a sense of well-being by exploring the history of the use of animals as healers in Germany and the United States, and the extent to which this concept has spread to other countries including Russia and Japan. As a result of qualitative research conducted over a period of three years in veterinary clinics, hospice, reading programs, search and rescue organizations, over fifty interviews and extensive review of existing literature on cultural studies of human-animal relations, we have found that, while similarities exist in the use of companion animals to enhance the human experience, the extent to which people anthropomorphize, adore, and even glorify animals differs specifically because of the cultures in which they were raised.

How animals have been incorporated into human society has much to do with how members of different cultures perceive and react to animals. Culture is the basis from which we form our beliefs, values, and how we act and respond to others and the world around us. The totality of culture is best described by d'Andrade as:

> learned systems of meaning, communicated by means of natural language and other symbols systems, having representational, directive, and affective functions, and capable of creating cultural entities and particular sense of reality. Through these systems of meaning groups of people adapt to their environment and structure interpersonal activities. (d'Andrade, 1984, p. 116)

Culture is a system of shared understandings, including values and beliefs that are communicated symbolically that help members of a group, community, or society perceive themselves, others, and their world. Culture is a way of experiencing the world, reflecting on it and reacting through systems of expression including language, art, traditions, and rituals, to mention a few. Moreover, cultures are not necessarily homogenous and certainly not static. Rather, diversity develops within cultures forming subcultures as part of the network of the larger culture including generational subcultures, gender, or work subcultures. Within cultures, key concepts and metaphors develop that express a community's core beliefs. For example, illnesses are often perceived as the enemy with whom we engage in battle. We make this clear in English with metaphors such as: "to fight an illness," "to battle a disease," "a war on cancer," "to take painkillers," to have a heart attack," and "symptoms flare up." Similar metaphors exist in German. When referring to health and our bodies, we may say "my body is my temple," which expresses the value of our bodies, the importance of health, and a reference to spirituality. Other people see their bodies as machines that, when broken, need to be fixed. When it comes to mental health, metaphors abound:

> A very well explored example is a conceptual metaphor on anger: the angry person is like a container about to burst. Within the framework of this structural metaphor we can understand a phrase like: smoke was coming out of him, prick him and he bursts, I almost exploded, he raised pressure, he erupted in insults, he is like boiled milk. This conceptual metaphor is recorded in Anglo-Saxon languages, Latin, Chinese, Japanese, Zulu, Slavic languages (Polish) and Hungarian. (Tajer, 2012, p. 489)

Cultures express their understandings of health by explaining causes of illness, "how it might be cured and who should be involved in the process" (Euromed-Info Bereiche, accessed March 9, 2017) through their unique metaphors.

Cultural concepts of health vary in the extent to which human intervention is believed to contribute positively. While in Western societies we tend to believe in the capabilities of medically trained professionals, in other parts of the world people struggle with Western notions of healing and may turn to supernatural powers to promote well-being. Japan presents an interesting case in point, where healthcare professionals acknowledge traditional beliefs as important to successful rehabilitation of individuals physically and mentally. The role of spiritual rituals plays an important part in Japan and it is common practice to express respect and reverence toward deities, supernatural forces, and ancestors. Japanese people do so by participating in traditional ceremonies, especially funerals and ancestor worship. Even though a majority of Japanese citizens do not consider themselves a member of a religious community, separating the spiritual from the scientific has become a topic of debate in the Japanese medical community. A scholar of Japanese medicine, Nagase, recounts:

> In 1999, the field of Japanese medical care witnessed a sharp increase in the number of academic publications on spirituality. Possibly, the increased focus on spirituality stemmed from the proposal, submitted between 1998 and 1999, to revise the "definition of health" by including the aspect of spirituality in the preamble to the World Health Organization (WHO)'s Charter. A revision in the definition was proposed at the 101st session of the WHO Executive Board by the WHO Regional Office for the Eastern Mediterranean, which included

members from Islamic member countries. The proposal sought to modify the definition of health by adding the underlined word as follows: "Health is a dynamic state of complete physical, mental, spiritual, and social well-being and not merely the absence of disease or infirmity." . . . The proposed definition differed from the original in two aspects. First, the concept of "health" was not identified as an individual's state of being healthy or ill but as a continuous and dynamic condition. Second, a spiritual dimension was added to the physical, mental, and social dimensions of health. The proposal was incorporated into the agenda of the 52nd World Health Assembly (WHA52) with 22 votes in favor, none against, and eight spoilt ballots. (Nagase, 2012, p. 71)

Currently the medical field is at odds with Japanese laymen, who consider spiritual balance an integral part of health, even if they are not affiliated with a particular religious community. Japan presents a clear example of the extent to which cultural foundations for concepts of health influence a person's feelings of well-being and the degree to which chosen therapies will "work" for that person holistically. Cultural attitudes can predict the patient's recovery utilizing certain methods and are more effective when the method coincides with cultural understandings.

Because cultural beliefs are an integral part of our understandings of health, much of what guides our ability to accept the healing powers of our companion animals is our cultural background. Our values and belief systems help form our enculturated concepts of health and health givers. The animal-as-healer narrative is revealed both in medical texts as well as in stories individuals tell of their emotional connection with animals. Relationships with animals are defined by people's beliefs and are subconsciously grounded in spirituality or cultural understandings about what goes on in an animal's mind. How do our narratives about our pets reflect our beliefs and definitions of identity and health? How are Western understandings different from non-Western alternatives? Besides exploring the history of the use of therapy animals in the West, its benefits and effects on the animals themselves, this book will take us to other parts of the world and explore various belief systems as well as differences in concepts of health among subcultures and co-cultures. Through the lens of human-animal interactions, we can gain insight into motivations that guide human understandings of what is right, moral, and healthy, how people assign meaning in life, and how cultural narratives affect the animals.

The chapters in this book are limited to studies conducted in complex societies, societies with which we, the authors, have been engaged and have studied for over a decade. Unfortunately, our review of the literature indicates that little has been written on the subject of small-scale societies. One study (Gray and Young, 2011) analyzed human investment in pets in sixty societies that included hunter-gatherers, horticulturalists, and pastoralists, for example. These, however, are not the focus of this book. Instead, we look at a pattern of development of animal contributions to human well-being that can be traced from England to other complex societies in the modern era.

DEFINING WELL-BEING

Cultural and religious belief systems worldwide form the foundation for variations in the human treatment of and attitudes toward animals. Combined with debates on proper interpretation of secular and non-secular texts and traditions, we see new values in societies developing as cultures cross-pollinate. The notion of cross-pollination of values and cultural inventory can be traced to such scholars as Franz Boas and his students and colleagues such as Alfred Kroeber, who introduced the idea of diffusion and acculturation respectively. Boas viewed culture as a culmination of loose threads woven to fit into their new cultural context (Hatch, 1973, pp. 57–58). Today the concept of diffusion is used to explain dominant cultural forms including beliefs and values that result from the introduction of foreign beliefs and values through domination, transformation, and acculturation. Diffusion and acculturation work together when elements of a culture are transformed, thus affecting in new ways how a community of people lives. Today, one would be hard-pressed to find a significant number of communities, cultures, and societies that have not been in some way touched by other societies.

Well-being is one such concept that has travelled and developed from one society to the next. In fact, it's popularity has grown to the point that people will speak of "a culture of well-being" in complex societies. A culture of well-being is a culture in which not only physical health, but emotional balance and mental stability (two concepts which also vary culturally in definitions) are achieved. A culture of well-being is generally accepted to be a culture that promotes the health and happiness of the individual.

The culture of well-being in the United States and in many Western societies is thriving, with variations in different parts of the world. Scholars of health and the social sciences describe wellness and well-being variously with few offering a universal application (Dodge et al., 2012, p. 222) or a rubric for analyzing culturally constructed views of well-being. That being said, there are elements across these varied definitions that are repeated including the notion of well-being as a subjective, culturally contextualized assessment of a person's quality of life. Often lacking in these definitions however, is reference to the dynamic nature of well-being. Marks offers one more possibility of a definition incorporating vibrancy:

> Well-being is not a beach you go and lie on. It's a sort of dynamic dance and there's movement in that all the time and actually it's the functuality of that movement which actually is true levels of well-being. (Marks in Dodge, 2012, p. 230)

While this definition speaks to the fluidity of well-being, it does not incorporate its essence: a subjective feeling that affects and is affected by the mind, the psyche of the individual. Petrzela (2016) in contrast, underscores the dimension of interconnectedness of mind and body in the concept of wellness, as something more than the absence of illness, one that involves human agency. Examples from her research demonstrate how the wellness movement in the United States is more than simply a victimization of consumers by corporations, that is, more than a "capitalist co-optation of wellness" (Petrzela, 2016), but a movement by a number of disenfranchised including those seeking better healing methods after feeling alienated by mainstream medicine (ibid.). In the United States, wellness culture offers liberation, even emancipation for women, helping to make lives more meaningful (ibid.). Engaging in the wellness culture involves a series of acts, externally guided but internally driven by the individual.

The Centers for Disease Control in the United States documents dimensions of well-being for a healthy society:

> There is no consensus around a single definition of well-being, but there is general agreement that at minimum, well-being includes the presence of positive emotions and moods (e.g., contentment, happiness), the absence of negative emotions (e.g., depression, anxiety), satisfaction with life, fulfillment and positive functioning. . . . In simple terms, well-being can be described as judging life positively and feeling good. . . . For public health purposes, physical well-being (e.g., feeling very healthy and full of energy) is also viewed as critical to overall well-being. Because well-being is subjective, it is typically measured with self-reports. [1]

We might add to this definition that well-being is defined through a conscious deliberate interaction of the individual with others and incorporating from culture those elements that are deemed therapeutic and healthy, including healthy activities and interactions. These cultural elements are borne out of sectarian and non-sectarian belief systems, from religious, medical, and traditional systems passed down and transformed from generation to generation orally and in written texts.

From a philosophical perspective, the incorporation of animals in our pursuit of well-being is, in a sense, a return toward nature rather than technology, technology being historically heralded as a means to a better life and human progress. The concept of progress through technological innovation is a concept that has defined development in many European countries and itself is characterized by manipulation and control over nature. While we continue our quest of progress by utilizing and controlling animals for our well-being, we also rely on their sometimes inexplicable and natural abilities to achieve comfort and healing. We find ourselves in the twenty-first century relying on a somewhat unscientific trust in animals for our progress in healing practices. It is only after the observation that animals can act as healers in human society, that we are beginning to uncover scientific explanations.

METHODOLOGY AND LITERATURE REVIEW

Many of the benefits we receive from animals are yet to be analyzed and so it makes sense to turn not only to the health sciences, but also to cultural narratives to better comprehend how animals contribute to human well-being. This book, therefore, approaches animal contributions to our well-being through scientific findings, historical texts and ethnographic research conducted over a period of three years, 2015–2017. Prior to conducting research, Institutional Review Board (IRB) approval was obtained to ensure that no one would be harmed. We explore the meaningfulness of animals in the lives of people in countries including Germany, Japan, Russia, and the United States through ethnographic fieldwork, in order to harvest the "insider's point of view," thus allowing critical beliefs and practices to emerge from the ethnographic encounter rather than imposing our own perspectives. This is called an *emic* perspective as opposed to an *etic* perspective, the latter being more analytical and removed from the experience (Hoey, 2014).

We have chosen to concentrate on Germany and the United States as it is in these countries that we have individually studied human-animal relations prior to discovering each other's research. Nommensen specializes in animal behavior modification, human-animal relations and veterinary science in Germany. Fujimura is an anthropologist studying human-animal relations (as well as marginalization of minority populations) in Russia, the United States and most recently, Japan. We found that these societies, with their unique histories and diverse populations, offered valuable examples of cultural differences in the treatment and uses of companion animals. Via ethnographic research, we were able to collect cultural narratives that exemplified complex and distinct understandings of the meaning of companion animals in daily lives.

Fundamental to the ethnographic approach is participant-observation research over an extended period of time. Such research was conducted in communities in Germany, Russia, and the United States, specifically in veterinary clinics, therapy training institutions, dog training organizations, search and rescue programs, assisted living homes, hospice program, and a library reading program. Interviews were conducted with members of all organizations as well as with members of the Japanese Embassy in Washington, DC, Japanese immigrants, and Japanese military families. The questions were open-ended to allow those interviewed not to feel limited in their responses.

Scholarly research focusing on cultural understandings of animals as healers is limited as is research on the history of therapy animals. Austrian zoologist Konrad Lorenz's work (1949) *So Kam der Mensch auf den Hund*, translated into English in 1954 under the title *Man Meets Dog,* can be seen as one of the earliest attempts to understand the history of canine incorporation into human society. However, his work was based mostly on his often unscientific thoughts on how this might have happened given his studies of animals in general. What is significant for this book is Lorenz's acknowledgment of the ability for dogs to experience human emotions and thereby connect with people and integrate into human society.

Since his seminal work, more has been written on the subject of the abilities of animals to serve us as workers, companions, and family members. The list of publications is extensive. With the surge in books on pets, the media has taken note. Scientific journalist Grimm (2014), in his book *Citizen Canine: Our Everyday Relationship with Cats and Dogs*, tells another version of Lorenz's story on how animals came into our lives and discusses the heightened status dogs and cats have achieved in Germany and numerous other complex societies. By interviewing animal rights advocates, rescue workers and military professionals, he demonstrates the professional roles that animals currently assume including that of police, warrior, and therapists. As such, animals have become much like human citizens with rights. The question of the extent of their rights remains debated.

Written histories of therapy animals are fewer. Articles are on the rise, however, definitive scholarship is scarce. More research exists on the types of therapy animals can perform, but scientific research on the subject is only recently coming to fruition. Greiffenhagen and Buck-Werner (2007) present a revised tome on animals as therapists, albeit in German. In this work, Greiffenhagen and Buck-Werner discuss the surge in animal therapy praxis, the problems such work encounters without proper legal ramifications and financial support. The work is a springboard for discussions on therapy work of Animal Assisted Therapy.

Few studies have resulted in cultural studies of animals-as-healers. One of the most influential works for our book on this subject is Pregowski's edited volume, *Companion Animals in Everyday Life: Situating Human-Animal Engagement within Cultures* (2016), in which scholars from fields such as anthrozoology, sociology, philosophy, history, political science, and psychology, to mention a few, examine "why people at a specific period in a culture think or act the way they do in relation to particular animals" (p. vii) in various parts of the world. What becomes clear throughout this book is the variety of animals that serve in complex ways to enhance the lives of humans. What animals mean to people, the extent to which they experience commodification or are perceived as reflections of ourselves is contextualized in a variety of countries including, but not limited to, the United States and countries in Asia and Eastern Europe. In particular, the research on Japan has informed the concept of the commodification of dogs in this book.

Cultural explorations of dogs in other societies are more frequent in scholarly literature than cross-cultural examinations of animals-as-healers. Of note is Skabelund's (2011) research on the symbolic power of canines in analyzing Japanese society. In his work, Skabelund sees the dog as a blank canvas on which metaphors of what it means to be human and to be Japanese evolve:

> People often define what it means to be human in relation to the nonhuman, so that animals have served as apt metaphors with which to assert the humanity and civilized nature of one's own group and the animality and barbaric character of "Others." (Skabelund, 2011, p. 16)

With his analysis of both the symbolic meaning and real existence of dogs in Japan, Skabelund reveals cultural attitudes about nation, race, class, and gender (p. 17).

Mondry (2015) similarly views the dog's body as "a site where body politics and politics are played out and where culture and nature, the sacred and the obscene, come together" (Mondry, 2015, p. 2). She does so by examining cultural representations of dogs in art, literature, lore, and film. Through her careful analysis, Mondry paints a picture that cuts to the essence of Russia, her soul, which is defined by social and political struggles through time. Indeed, if anything may serve as a vehicle to capture the Russian soul, it is her literature. The symbolic gravitas of dog characters in Russian literature reflects and illuminates varying notions throughout Russian history of spirituality, class, morality and justice. For this book, Mondry's work launches the discussion of Russia's perceptions of dogs and modern uses in therapy work.

The literature on which much of our research is based is just that, a basis. From here the authors expand on the scholarship readily available to offer a comprehensive discussion on animals as contributors to human well-being in culturally contextualized settings. Furthermore, we take from our professional praxis with animals in such venues as veterinary clinics and human health facilities, experience that broaden our understanding of the potential for human-animal engagement and mutually reinforcing benefits.

OUTLINE

We begin in chapter 1, "Animals as Therapists: How We Discovered Them and What They Do" with a historical examination of therapeutic work utilizing animals in the West. As will become clear, animals have enriched therapeutic work since as far back as the ninth century AD. However, their role in such a capacity has changed significantly. While initially animals served on the fringes in a supportive role as, for example, in helping to distract patients from painful procedures, today animals take on a roll of active therapist. The scope of their work is large, be it as a service animal (for people with physical or emotional challenges) or as a visiting therapist for senior citizens in assisted living homes, or as an assistant working to help children at the elementary level to develop reading skills. By studying the evolution of animals as therapists, we discover the multitude of possibilities for enhancing human well-being through human-animal interaction. The scope of their abilities offers great potential for human society and opens doors for human therapists which, without the animal at their side, would have remained closed. In today's increasingly complex and stressful world, there is an increase in corresponding psychiatric illnesses including burnout, depression, anxiety, and post-traumatic stress disorder (PTSD). Such illnesses are obviously profiting from work with therapy animals, a fact that has become clear in recent scholarship and through our extensive interviews with doctors, therapy teams, and patients.

Beyond our own contemporary experiences with the integration of animals into our medical practices and institutions, there is insight to be gained from a study of similar practices historically and culturally. And so, chapter 2, "Cultural Foundations of Human-Animal Relations," takes us to a deeper level, beyond the confines of Germany and the United States. In this chapter, we explore the relationship of humans and animals and the use of animals as contributors to human well-being by examining the role of spirituality in contributing to concepts of well-being with a particular focus on Japan and Russia. In both these countries, animals are cherished as companions and co-workers, but the way in which they are utilized differs depending on each country's unique history, belief systems, and traditions. In order to understand the development of human-animal relations in each country, narratives significant to the countries were selectively chosen. In Russia, we begin by examining one of Russia's cultural treasures, her folk narratives and literature. In Japan, we look more closely at rituals that guide the lives of people and a developing urban consumer society. For both societies, outcomes from interviews with urban, middle class Japanese and Russian citizens inform much of our findings.

At the forefront of integrating animals as healers are countries that have turned to understanding animal behavior and communication. In chapter 3, "Well-Being through Communication with and about Our Pets" we explore the importance of understanding animal communication in order not only to achieve better results in therapy, but also to ensure the well-being of the animals. This chapter discusses animal-human communication and miscommunication based on communication and culture theories that form a framework for analysis of collected narratives. We begin this chapter with examples of miscommunication that occur as a result of an inclination to assume human-like reactions from animals. This inclination is driven by a desire to achieve a sense of well-being which we acquire when we feel emotionally connected to those around us. We achieve connection to others when we communicate effectively, deeply, and positively. Miscommunications due to anthropomorphizing is largely the result of our contradictory relationship with our pets: on the one hand we see them much as we do material possessions and on the other we assign them social status and personhood. These contradictory relationships affect both human and animal emotional well-being.

It is in chapter 3 that we include a discussion of how dogs perceive the world. Both Fujimura and Nommensen are extensively involved in training dogs to track and trail scents, and to engage in search and rescue operations. In doing so, we, as many dog behaviorists and trainers will agree, find that the dog's incredible sense of smell has not been sufficiently studied to address in a comprehensive way, how dogs live, think, and react because of all that they smell. Indeed, books have been written on the subject, but they tend to end with a discussion of how much more we need to learn to truly appreciate all the ramifications and possibilities. This is, to a large extent, due to the fact that what a dog can smell, we cannot. In training for tracking we have witnessed a dog's ability to track another animal's or human's trail even if others have tread on the same trail, and even if it is a number of days old.

Scent is the most primitive of our, human and dog alike, senses: "its connections go directly to the more primitive, and emotional, parts of the brain" (McConnell, 2007, p. 105). McConnell adds: "I often wonder if we could be using scent more effectively to communicate with our dogs" (McConnell, 2007). Indeed, we do communicate via our scent, only most of what we are communicating is probably subconsciously for a dog can tell from our scent not only who we are, but where we have been, what we have just eaten, what mood we are in and so much more.

To explain the way in which we communicate subconsciously with our dogs, chapter 3 engages the reader to consider the "Rucksack Effect," a term coined by Nommensen to help us understand in particular how dogs read us and respond to us. This concept will be addressed again in chapter 5 as we reveal best practices in working with animals. By acknowledging that dogs can perceive this invisible rucksack which we carry through life, we come closer to understanding our dogs' motivations and behaviors through which, in turn, we can attain emotional stability. Research narratives collected from Nommensen's veterinary practice, illuminate the complexity of animal perceptions whereby we arrive at the ultimate insight, the healing potential of close contact with animals.

In chapter 4, "Mutual Benefits through Human-Animal Contact and Training: What Science and Personal Narratives Tell," we dig into the ways in which animals enrich our human existence and moreover, ways in which we can enrich the well-being of our animals in similar ways. As its focus, this chapter concentrates on the dynamic relationship which we hold with our non-human animals and the extent to which our lives improve due to our cohabitation with companion animals. Animals are motivators—they keep us active, flexible, and also mentally fit. Through their open and nonjudgmental manner of approaching humans, they give us the feeling of unconditional acceptance. These characteristics render them diplomats and icebreakers in our social surroundings. But why have certain animals (dogs and cats, for example) made it into our human social surroundings while others have not? This question will also be investigated in this chapter.

Finally, we will turn to how humans influence the well-being and health of our companion animals via cohabitation. Our effects on our animals can be both positive and negative. Complete veterinary care, extensive selections on pet food and care products as well as pet day care are just a few options we deem positive contributions to our pets' lives. However poor communication, disposition or temperament of the animal can lead to grave complications for both human and non-human partners. This too will be discussed.

Chapter 5, "The Animal's Perspective," uncovers the hidden lives of dogs and offers insight into senses which often go neglected and impede the balance of human-animal teamwork. Companion animals, in particular dogs, perceive their environment and social contexts differently than we humans do and differently from how we tend to think they do. In this chapter, the author familiarizes the reader with this foreign world which our animals inhabit. While we often believe we know our pets better than anyone can, we believe that the process of truly understanding our pets is an ongoing process. Nommensen hopes that with this chapter, all those who share their homes with or in some way work with animals as pets, therapists, or other, will widen and open their horizons of knowledge and potential understanding. As we have seen throughout this book, dogs, with their similarities to us, have managed to acclimate harmoniously and lovingly to our lives and to enter into our hearts. However, as discussed in chapter three, our cohabitation is not free of miscommunication and resulting conflicts. These conflicts need to be taken under a microscope so that we may come to understand our companion animals in a different light and to see them as the complete, exceptional, and individual non-human beings that they are.

WHY THIS BOOK AND WHY NOW?

We, the authors of this book, met in the context of our personal and professional exposure to the German and United States military. As our lives intersected, we found that we had much more in common, namely our research and involvement in training and working with service and therapy animals. While our lives intersected professionally, we also found that there was much work to be done to better understand the nature of animals as they enhance our lives in a variety of cultural contexts and, in particular, in serving the military. Especially as we watch our friends and colleagues go to war, live in war zones or return with serious physical and emotional injuries, we cannot stand by and not share what we know about animals-as-healers. Moreover, as our family members, students, and peers leave the comfort of their homes, we felt the need to share the significance of understanding other cultures' beliefs in the value of animals from a social scientific perspective. A returning veteran, Major Matt Lampert, who served and suffered in Afghanistan helped to confirm the importance of our work in sharing his experiences with dogs in a war zone:

> As a wartime tool and asset these dogs were awesome. Often dogs were trained to do different things (track, sniff out bomb making material and explosives and to bite as well). Dogs for us were tremendously useful tools to help defend friendly forces from harm as well as to do our jobs. However, there is more to the story than that. MWDs and their human dog handlers paid a huge price in terms of loss during the time period I was in Afghanistan (2010–2012). For me the dogs, and for that matter all the other animals, I encountered helped us to stay centered. Animals are inherently innocent and they don't harbor ill intentions (unlike many of the humans we encountered). I enjoyed on a patrol seeing the dog and dog handler be able to play and get some shade etc. Those kinds of moments remind you that life has more to offer than just danger and death. My first deployment to Afghanistan there were three little kittens who lived by the back door of the kitchen and early in the morning when it was cool out, they would come out and just be kittens. I used to love just watching them for ten minutes or so roll around and attack each other etc. They would get a little pet from me before I had to head out and focus on the task at hand of planning for a raid that night. (Lampert, 2017)

The work of animals in the military does not end abroad. As veterans return, the ability for dogs to help those managing their lives with a loss of limbs or those managing post-traumatic stress find comfort in the help that dogs can provide.

Our hope is that through this book, readers will develop a deeper understanding of the wide-ranging benefits that animals have brought and continue to bring to humans, both at home and abroad. We also hope to help readers, both laymen and scholars alike, become more curious about the complexities of human-animal interaction and the uniqueness of their own relationships to animals that are not simply personal but, to a large extent, dependent on culture. From how we define well-being to how we utilize animals to contribute to our well-being and to what degree we take the well-being of the healer-pet into account, these are only some of the distinguishing features we must understand fully to allow us to build on our relationship with animals in mutually beneficial ways. We hope to motivate more scholarly discussion on cross-cultural comparisons as animals become healers not just in a few nations, but globally.

NOTE

1. http://www.cdc.gov/hrqol/well-being.htm. Accessed May 24, 2016.

Chapter One

Animals as Therapists: How We Discovered Them and What They Do

⸙

HOW WE DISCOVERED THEM

When we think of therapy animals, we might envision a little dog helping a child with special needs. However, the list of kinds of animal-therapists extends beyond the imagination as do the animals' capabilities. In this chapter, we will discover the variety of animal-therapists in their historical contexts. We begin with a look at the major events in the treatment and rehabilitation of humans with physical and psychological challenges that led to contemporary uses of animals as healers in Europe and the United States. Throughout our explorations, we will create a taxonomy of the variety of animal therapy programs as they are known today and end by addressing briefly what we owe our animals if indeed we value them as contributors to our well-being.

While we tend to think of animal therapy as a rather new aspect of medical treatment, we find that quite to the contrary, animals have been utilized to enhance our well-being and health for over one thousand years. The first documentation of animal therapy dates back to the ninth century. Animals at that time were not specifically prescribed to work with people as much as people with challenges were given work with animals to structure their day, and to enable them to become active and contributing members of society. Engaging in animal husbandry allowed individuals who might otherwise have been marginalized to be assimilated. As a result, they received therapeutic benefits we today recognize as outcomes of Pet Therapy, including decreased feelings of isolation and increased socialization.

Acceptance of psychiatric and developmental challenges as medical issues was slow to develop historically. It was not until the Middle Ages that hospitals for people with disabilities were established. However, such hospitals did not lead to integration of the patients in society, rather, to the isolation of them. Many of today's medically defined challenges, such as autism, were considered to be "the devil's work" and patients were segregated and confined rather than treated.

In the eighteenth century the tide began to turn with the formation of the first sanatoriums which sought to help people labeled with psychosocial and developmental disabilities. In 1792 the Society of Friends created a clinic called the "York Retreat" for psychiatric patients. The goal of this clinic was to facilitate independent living accompanied by therapy. The founder of the York Retreat, William Tuke, transformed the former insane and inhumane asylums into a more humane institution with Christian underpinnings. Located in the quiet countryside, it beckoned people to relax in its gardens and be treated as guests rather than prisoners by, for example, allowing them to wear their own clothes and stroll freely and at their leisure. Also, part of the program was the incorporation of small animals, who not only acted to distract but were also utilized in therapy sessions to motivate the guests to care for them and become active participants rather than passive patients in their treatment and personal growth.[1]

Unfortunately, this method of care was increasingly abandoned as Western society became industrialized and modern methods of analysis and medical research took over despite the fact that the results with animal therapy had been found to be effective. Patients were once again housed in institutions with minimal physical, let alone psychological support, often neglected and even abused. Special therapy sessions involving pets were not considered a viable approach. It was not until a doctor, Levinson, in 1961 by chance picked up, where Tuke left off, that animal therapy was reintroduced as a means to rehabilitation and developmental support. We will return to Levinson later in our discussion of the twentieth century.

However, experimentation with animals as helpers in treatment plans continued. In Germany, for example, the first sanatorium in Germany (Bielefeld, est. 1867) was built on an agricultural estate as it was thought that people suffering from epilepsy could be distracted from their seizures by interacting with farm animals to strengthen and enhance the healing process (Schöll, 2015).

The next animal therapy intervention that became popular was in the United States in 1919 when dogs were brought to patients at Saint Elizabeth Hospital in Washington, DC, to help soldiers returning from the battlefields of World War I with emotional and psychological challenges. This came about due to a suggestion by the then U.S. Secretary of the Interior, Franklin K. Lane, who had been inspired by the veterans of World War I who told of how dogs were a great comfort to them when they encountered them. As soon as dogs were at the hospital, it became clear that Lane's idea was a success. Dogs were found to aid not only emotionally by comforting patients, but also physically as men suffering from shell shock were able to regain their balance with a dog at their side. Lane's vision proved to be a success and the hospital exists to this day (Hassink and van Dijk, 2006, p. 315).

After Lane's experiment, it took another World War to bring the dogs back. Toward the end of World War II in 1944, doctors assigned to the Air Force Convalescent Hospital in New York advocated the use of both farm animals and dogs to help soldiers who were suffering psychologically from traumatic experiences. Unlike previous experiments, patients were permitted to bring their own dogs, care for them and train them at the facility. Any patient who wished to be a part of the program either brought their own dog or was given a dog. As a result of this program, the grounds of the hospital were populated by a variety of animals including cows, sheep, and goats with whom patients were encouraged to work. Inside there was an abundance of wagging tails adding to the general feeling of content (Rusk 1972).

It was during this period that doctors began to move beyond merely physically accommodating patients to offering psychiatric support. Prior to this, disabled veterans had been given only the most basic care without mental stimulation during their convalescence. In 1944 the Pawling Center in Tucson, Arizona, was established. It was "a combination of a hospital, a country club, a school, a farm, a vocational training centre, a resort and a little bit of home . . . Pawling was the first of twelve such centres the Air Force opened during World War II . . . we had between four and five hundred patients there, beat-up boys from battlefronts all over the world" (Rusk, 1972, pp. 68–72). As veterans became more mentally engaged, health care professionals witnessed an acceleration of veterans' convalescence and reintegration into society. Other rehabilitation centers soon followed, offering activities and programs to support psychological recovery as well as physical therapy.

After the success of the Pawling Centre, pets began to spread beyond veterans' hospitals to those for children. In 1948 Samuel B. "Rollo" Ross realized his teenage dream of bringing animals to the boarding school experience. Initially a small school in Putnam County, New York, that encouraged a love of the environment and community, "Green Chimneys" became a school for children and youth with special needs. Among other therapeutic opportunities, admitted children were, and continue to be, tasked with caring for farm animals to encourage each child to develop skills and foster their ability to be successful academically, socially, and emotionally. While work, such as that which continues to be used at Green Chimneys, utilizes animals to help people establish skills, find a purpose, and support reentry into society, it is not what we term Animal Assisted Therapy. Rather such work is today called "Farm Therapy" or "Green Therapy."[2]

Our contemporary understanding of Animal Assisted Therapy came to life with the ideas of psychologist Boris Levinson in New York in 1961. By accident, Levinson discovered the capabilities of dogs as co-therapists in his own practice which focused on youth. Levinson himself describes this milestone in modern animal therapy:

> Early one morning, Jingles was lying at my feet while I was busily writing at my desk when the doorbell rang. Jingles was never permitted into my office when I expected patients, but this day no one was due until several hours later. Jingles followed me to the door where we were greeted by a very distraught parent and child—several hours early for their appointment. This child had already been exposed to a long stretch of unsuccessful therapy. Hospitalization had been recommended. The appointment with me had been set up for a diagnostic interview, at which time I would decide whether or not to take on as a patient this boy who showed increasing symptoms of withdrawal. While I greeted the mother, Jingles ran right up to the child and began to lick him. Much to my surprise, the child showed no fright but instead cuddled up to the dog and began to pet him. When the mother wanted to separate the boy and dog, I signalled her to leave them alone. Before the end of the interview with the parent, the child expressed the desire to return and play with the dog. With such auspicious beginnings, the treatment of Johnny commenced. For several subsequent sessions, he played with the dog, seemingly unaware of my presence. However, we held many conversations during which he was so intent upon the dog that he seemed not to be listening to me although his replies were coherent. Eventually, some of the affection elicited by the dog spilled over onto me and I was consciously included in the play. Slowly, we came to the establishment of a sound rapport which made it possible to work out Johnny's problems. Some of the credit for the eventual rehabilitation of Johnny must go to Jingles who was a most willing co-therapist. (Levinson, 1969, p. 59)

From then on Levinson included his dog in his sessions with this boy. The stage would be set by allowing the boy to play and cuddle freely without interference. At first it appeared as if the dog was the therapist with Levinson watching from the sidelines. After some sessions, the boy began to accept Levinson and allowed him to take part in the fun. In time, Levinson was able to take more of a leadership role in the sessions, ultimately permitting him to give the necessary conventional therapy in the presence of the dog.

Levinson's work was critical to the incorporation of animals in psychological therapy. In 1962 health scientist Siegel published an article on the positive effects animals can have on humans. He referenced the York Retreat and further described findings at the Speyer Hospital for Animals, a veterinary clinic, at which staff noted positive effects of animals on their owners. Siegel was of the opinion that animals are effective as co-therapists because they approach humans regardless of their appearance, status, or illness. With their nonjudgmental disposition, animals can access the ailing human more quickly than another human might:

> The animal does not judge but offers a feeling of intense loyalty to persons who need that feeling. It is not frightening or demanding, nor does it expose its master to the ugly strain of constant criticism. It provides its owner with the chance to feel important knowing that the pet's dependency is on him. (Siegel, 1962, p. 1046)

To this day, his statement remains the basis for which we turn to animals in therapy.

Contributions to our scientific knowledge on the subject of animal therapy increased after this. In the 1970s, Sam and Elizabeth O'Leary Corson opened an animal laboratory at the psychiatric clinic at Ohio State University. Their main focus was to observe and understand canine behavior in a variety of situations with the hypothesis that their findings would enrich their understanding of adolescent behavior. In 1977, they began a study with a variety of breeds. However, their results also led to a better understanding of the benefits to both patients and staff:

> They introduced the dogs to 50 hospitalized psychiatric patients, most of whom had failed to respond adequately to traditional forms of therapy. . . . The introduction of Pet-facilitated Psychotherapy exerted significant favourable effects on the "esprit de corps" of the ward. It led to extensive positive social interactions, not only on the part of the patient being treated, but also on the part of the other patients. It improved staff-patient interactions. . . . The availability of a large assortment of well trained dogs of different breeds made it possible to match the personality and the disorder of a given patient with a dog with which the patient could best interact . . . it is difficult to identify the factors that have contributed to the improvement of a patient in a hospital. . . . All that can be said at this time is that preliminary results appear to be encouraging, particularly since the patients selected for the study were those who had reached a plateau of nonresponding to all the traditional forms of therapy. (Corson et al., 1977, pp. 61–72)

With this experiment, it becomes clear that the use of an animal can improve results and progress of therapy sessions. Patients find themselves capable of opening up and can be receptive to new therapeutic approaches and medical professionals. Both the medical staff and patients benefitted in this instance.

Soon after, Friedmann (1980) began her pioneering studies on the relationship between pet ownership and human health. She observed ninety-two patients who had experienced a heart attack or angina. Fifty-three of the patients had pets, the remaining patients were without. After one calendar year, fourteen patients died, but only three of these had pets. Other data recorded of these patients, such as blood values, nutrition, or smoking habits, did not offer any significant differences which could explain the deaths. It was concluded that pet ownership was a significant factor in maintaining and improving health among those surviving (Friedmann, 1980, p. 307).

The results of these studies prompted further investigations on the positive effects of animals on humans. Ultimately it was confirmed that animals can have significant positive effects on the physical and emotional well-being (Beck and Katcher, 1996). One outcome of these findings was the Delta Organization in Portland in 1977 whose mission was and continues to be to disseminate information on the benefits of Pet Therapy and to encourage training and certification for animals who work as therapists. Today they are better known as Pet Partners in the United States and internationally work under the umbrella organization, the International Association of Human-Animal Interaction Organizations (IAHAIO) with its main office in Washington, DC. IAHAIO serves to unite therapy research organizations from around the world, including the Society for Companion Animal Studies in the United Kingdom, the Research Circle of Pets in Society (Forschungskreis Heimtiere in der Gesellschaft) in Germany, and the Society for the Study of Human Animal Relations in Japan, to mention a few.

The mission of the Delta Organization was emulated in Europe where dogs soon began visiting medical facilities, nursing homes, and hospice. Biologist Gerda Wittman was one of the first to begin animal therapy programs in Austria in 1985. With a number of assistants and despite initial difficulties convincing officials of the feasibility of animals as therapists, she established an animal-visitation program at a geriatric care facility: the Geriatriezentrum in Lainz. With the advent of her organization, the awareness of Pet Therapy and research on the subject rose among medical scientists and practitioners in Europe. By 1997 the organization was firmly established and is currently located at the veterinary school at the University of Vienna with a database of research for world-wide access. Furthermore, this university now offers specialized higher education courses on the subject of therapy dogs.

In 1987, a veterinarian, Brigitte von Rechenberg, founded a club "Tiere Helfen Menschen" (Animals Help People) in Germany based on the principles of Pet Partners in the United States. The goal of this organization was to standardize education and training methods as proposed by Pet Partners. To this day, however, small independent training groups tend to set their own standards. Attempts to nationally unify educational and examination standards have failed.

To summarize, early on in Western history, animals were utilized as structuring devices in helping humans socialize and integrate into society more easily. At the center were humans who needed to be helped and animals were a means to an end, to be replaced or discarded when they had fulfilled their role. Animals were chosen by type, not as individuals who possess unique personalities and qualities: "the decision as to which animal was used was less about whether or not a specific animal matched the patient, which animal should or should not be used, but more about which would fit the space, the model or the financial and personal condition" (Niepel, 1998, p. 60). Animals were seen as functional instruments much like a prescription or a tool a doctor could exchange for another. The idea that animals can be partners in therapy, that the pairing of patient and animal is of significant value became evident only in the later 1980s.

Since the 1980s, in European countries and in the United States, the variety of therapy groups has exploded. Unfortunately, because this explosion remains unstructured, there is a lack of professional cohesion, exchange of information, and networking opportunities. Only slowly in the twenty-first century are we witnessing symposia dedicated to bringing together Pet Therapists and researchers. During our research, it became clear that all the professionals (therapists, behaviorists, trainers for therapy pets, etc.) are convinced of a need for a unified forum in order to foster the exchange of ideas, and to grow in knowledge and expertise, rather than languish and repeat one's mistakes in training and practice.

In 2004, the European Society for Animal Assisted Therapy (ESAAT) in Vienna attempted to unify the education of Pet Therapists based on the most up-to-date research, albeit without any legal foundation. This failed. A further goal by ESAAT is to achieve official recognition of Pet Therapy so as to establish a standardization of the field and profession. Not only would it help in regulating quality of performance of professional Pet Therapists (volunteer or otherwise) but official regulation could help in informing patients and possibly lead to therapy insurance coverage.

ANIMAL ASSISTED THERAPY TODAY

A Focus on Dogs

Animal Assisted Therapy thus developed slowly, but today is acknowledged by many health care professionals as a successful technique to assist regular therapy to promote the well-being of certain individuals. As the name suggests, Animal Assisted Therapy today occurs when a therapist, trained in her respective field such as psychology, speech therapy, or occupational therapy, works with a patient with the added support of an animal. As an assistant to the therapist, the animal does not work alone, but with direction from his or her human handler, so that animal and human function as a therapeutic team. To arrive at the level of actually working together, both the handler and animal will have undergone a process of training and testing to be certified as a team.

Not all animals are suited for this kind of work. Some dogs are naturals, whereas others cannot be forced to do this kind of work. In training dogs for therapy, we select dogs that match the specific job they are expected to do. For example, if the therapist is working with a child suffering from spasms, it is ideal if the dog is one that is not easily excited by erratic movements. The goal for such a child is to strengthen emotional and cognitive functions and the ability to carry out necessary activities that help the child become more independent, ultimately improving the child's personal sense of well-being.

The authors have found work with hospice patients as well as in nursing homes and rehabilitation centers to be extremely rewarding for both patient and handler. In these areas, a variety of animals have been utilized including, but not limited to, dogs, cats, rabbits, and horses. What is important is that the animal possess a calm, reliable disposition. Pack or herd animals in particular lend themselves well for this kind of work as they are masters of communication stemming from their need to survive in a group. Through nonverbal communication, these animals, among their pack or herd, are successful diplomats and resolvers of conflict.

Humans communicate both verbally and non-verbally with nonverbal communication manifesting the largest part of the communication process. It can happen as soon as you meet a person for the first time, when you automatically, possibly subconsciously, judge a person to be likeable or not without having even spoken to the person. Both in German and in English, we call this a gut feeling (*Bauchgefühl*). In seconds we read gestures, facial twitches and even smell to form an opinion. Nonverbal communication allows us to react quickly, to measure our responses and to ensure the best outcome in the interaction, much like animals do.

By understanding this basic tendency to use nonverbal communication in animals, we are able to train them to engender a special bond between patient and animal that helps the patient achieve a particular goal. Given its size and trainability, dogs, unlike other animals, have an advantage as a service provider and therapy partner. They can further function as physical support, help with motor exercises (such as holding fur to relax or strengthen muscles) and affect the individual psyche.

In psychological counseling, pets may initiate the session and facilitate communication by putting everyone at ease. As a result of our interviews, we learned from a number of therapists that patients, especially children, at times believed the animal to be the therapist as opposed to the psychologist or other human therapist present (such as speech therapist, occupational therapist, etc.). Patients may turn to the dog rather than the human to discuss their concerns, fears, trauma, thereby making the information indirectly available to the therapist. It is sometimes difficult to discern which therapist, human or animal, is in the leading role! One therapist (N. M. interview, June 4, 2016) specializing in suicide prevention finds that her patients, both current and past, come to her office specifically to speak to her dog. To support this need, she created a space in which patients can also have privacy and feel safe. Engaging with an animal can be a first step in opening up to the human therapist.

Patients suffering from post-traumatic stress have taken to Animal Assisted Therapy as animals can help ease stress and fears. In a study by Brickel (1986) it was found that tension and relaxation are incompatible. In the presence of an animal that causes a relaxed state a patient may never have a once expected panic attack.

In another study, Brickel (1982) found that animals support continuity in therapeutic contexts. Especially when clients feel uncomfortable about attending therapy sessions, when animals are present, they are more likely to return and continue with therapy than when there are no animals. The animals allow for positive emotions to outweigh the negative experiences, leading to a desire to persist.

Equally important is the animal's ability to elicit communication and thereby facilitate dialogue between the therapist and the client. Even traumatic experiences can be discussed due to the mere presence of an animal. An animal helps a patient to take control of the situation, at times beginning with a patient speaking directly to the animal before venturing into a conversation with the therapist, thus making it easier to talk about a taboo subject, for example (Wells/Perrine, 2001).

A further study on the subject of Animal Assisted Therapy demonstrated the positive effects of pets on our ability to de-stress, be less judgmental and release our inhibitions. We do this by communicating with our pets much like we might with a young child, by using a higher pitch, lower volume, and slower speech. We often end our communication in a question to soften the message. By addressing animals in a milder manner than we might an adult, we are appeased, less prone to judgment, feel less judged, and enjoy the sense of empathy an animal seems to provide (Katcher and Beck, 1989). The way in which we communicate affects how we feel and think.

In an interview with therapist Daniela E. Hahn (2017) who works primarily with physically and emotionally challenged children, she told of her work in tandem with her dogs Momo and Leon who are both certified as therapy dogs. Each day leads to new discoveries: "My dogs motivate the children like you would not believe, simply by their presence. Sometimes I envy the ease with which they reach the children whereas I need to make a bigger effort to achieve similar results." She offers as an example David, a bright boy who suffers from tetraspasticism. His four limbs are constantly tense hindering him from coordinated movement. He uses a wheelchair. The tension also affects his breathing and speech. David is especially motivated by the dogs and upon entering immediately talks: "When do we start? When is Momo coming? What about Leon?" Hahn continues: "And so the minute he walks in speech bubbles out of him and his mood is almost always good. Most children feel that they are responsible for the dog's mood and so try to be positive around them. As one child once told me: 'Momo came extra to me today so I need to be good'" (Hahn, 2017).

But that is not all that her dogs provide. They help strengthen children's use of muscles and develop physiological abilities such as holding and petting, inhaling and exhaling, fluency of speech, and stimulate their ability to focus. David has developed his ability to concentrate longer, his breathing has slowed down helping his fluency of speech: "Leon and Momo have even motivated David to get out of his wheelchair and to take his first steps! If that doesn't speak for animal assisted therapy" (Hahn, 2017).

Animals accept patients without any judgment. Unlike humans, they do not send automatic signals that might deter a patient from opening up. A human, while expressing sympathy via speech, might unknowingly nonverbally be, for any number of reasons, sending a message of apathy toward the subject. Perhaps the listener had heard about it before. Perhaps they do not feel it is important. Perhaps they do not mean to send that signal and yet the inhibiting message is received.

When such unintentional communication occurs between the therapist and patient, progress is unlikely to occur. Children are extremely sensitive to these situations and so animals, who are direct in their communication, are less confusing to them:

> For example, I can reach my patients through the dog by asking the patient an indirect question such as—"Momo would like to know how you feel today . . . Leon thinks that your arm is hurting. Is that correct?" And so, I can ask things without speaking directly to the children, which is incredibly helpful. Some children like those living with Autism, do not enjoy direct conversation. (Hahn, 2017)

It is important to keep in mind, however, that not all dogs desire the job of therapist and that it is essential to train both human and dog, if the team is deemed willing and able: "You will not be able to achieve positive results if the human is motivated but the dog is too jumpy" (Hahn, 2017).

Another component of Animal Assisted Therapy is the ability for the animal to have an effect on patients who are exhausted by the amount of conventional therapy they have undergone. Patients may feel hopeless, unmotivated to continue or to try new options. Animals can function as the initial motivator in such situations and can work as mediators between the patient and therapist. Prothmann (2012, in Wohlfahrt et al., 2013) studied children and youth with psychological challenges and discovered that the sessions with animals were less stressful than when the animals were absent. Patients' perception of themselves as individuals grew and they felt more accepted and understood by the therapist in the presence of animals. Once a connection with patient and therapist is established, therapy sessions are more likely to be successful (Prothmann, 2012, in Wohlfahrt et al., 2013). The perception that a therapist is authentic and cares leads to trust, an essential therapeutic component (Rogers, 1973), is facilitated by the presence of animals.

Equine-Assisted Therapy Today

Equine therapy has also proven to promote well-being of people with physical and mental challenges. It is a form of therapy that can help to strengthen both the mental and physical abilities of the patient as it entails active engagement, such as caring for the animal, stable maintenance, riding on or off lead, even vaulting, depending on the individual's capabilities. Besides physical strengthening, horses can aid people suffering from trauma, depression, and psychiatric disorders.[3]

Riding therapy has become popular in Europe and the United States. It is considered to be an effective tool for improving mobility with sufferers of cerebral palsy, paralysis, multiple sclerosis, and strokes, to mention a few. Germany is a leader in the field of riding therapy with an impressive increase in therapeutic riding centers over the past twenty years (Gäng, 1992; Scheidhacker, 1996). As with dogs, the disposition and physical aspect of the horse can lend itself to successful therapy work: Horses are naturally curious about humans and, depending on the horse, welcome interaction. Culturally in the West, the horse is respected and perceived as beautiful, making it an acceptable animal for therapy.

However, the ability for a horse to aid in therapy goes beyond cultural beliefs surrounding the horse or its disposition and furriness. Unlike traditional physical therapy and rehabilitation with machines, the horse's motion is three-dimensional: right/left, forward/backward, and up/down. The swinging motion of a horse, which is identical to the swinging motion of a human walking, is transferred to the patient, stimulating and strengthening the gluteal, back, and abdominal muscles. Unlike the capabilities of conventional therapy, which offers more focused stimulation, in riding therapy the entire body is engaged. Changes in speed and direction help decrease fear of motion (as witnessed among trauma patients), increase self and spatial perception, and increase relaxation. A horse's variety of gaits (walk, trot, canter . . . we tend not to gallop during therapy, although this is a fourth gait) have a multitude of effects on the rider. For example, with the walk—a four-step pace in which one leg moves at a time—a rider experiences a concentrated release of muscle tension.

Moreover, horses communicate with their riders thereby reaching nonverbal patients who have felt isolated from peers. They react to weight and posture changes as well as to the mood of the rider by changing their own behavior. Anyone who has worked with horses knows well the importance of reading or feeling their body language to develop mutual trust and patience in order to move forward (or backward) flowingly. Working with horses requires mindfulness and awareness of all that is going on between the bodies and psyches.

The development of trust begins on the ground, prior to mounting. Patients must learn how to approach the horse appropriately but with an open mind and confidence, as well as a willingness to lead and be led. Depending on the role, leader or led, feelings and reactions are evoked, resulting in becoming self-aware. Working with horses can lead to reawakening a presence of mind, adaptability, and teamwork (Rockenbauer, 2010). Horses selected for working with humans have helped motivate patients to heal, increase their ability to concentrate over longer periods of time, and increase their willingness to correct their own mistakes (Kröger, 1989, p. 11).

However, as mentioned above, riding is not the sole aspect of equine therapy that serves in the rehabilitation and support of patients. When possible, the physical labor involved in caring for a horse can prove beneficial, especially for children. Children who have a difficult time concentrating or completing tasks, improve when challenged to care for the horse they have become attached to. Moreover, because much of the work they do involves other children, they can learn from one another and foster socialization skills. In ideal situations, groups of children are structured with care bringing together individuals with different strengths and weaknesses. For example, it would be impractical to place all children with impaired speech in the same group. More learning can happen when those who struggle in one area find leadership among those who do not take the same challenge.

Riding therapy can be an effective tool in helping people with communication disturbances. Individuals, and in particular children with speech disorders as well as children who have difficulty discerning right from left, may tend to misalign the order of letters or words in a sentence. As riding students learn right from left while controlling the horse, they can be tasked with building words to form grammatical sentences. The movement patterns of the various gates of a horse have a relaxing effect and are similar to our rhythms we use to speak. Relaxation and rhythm are key elements in improving speech. While riding, children learn to maintain a rhythm in a relaxed state thereby developing speech.

Equine therapy is considered by many to be truly miraculous. Those working with the human and horse have seen children develop in unforeseen ways, helping them become happier and more balanced individuals: "It is as if the horse knows what is needed to bring the best out in my son . . . he learned to smile doing this" one mother tells (J. S., 2017).

PET THERAPY

Unlike Animal Assisted Therapy, Pet Therapy is not woven into a session with a health professional. Rather, through visitations with a human handler, the certified animal is escorted to individuals who would benefit from the animal as in reading programs or to individuals in need of some comfort in personal homes, nursing facilities, rehabilitation centers, hospitals, and hospice. Especially in Germany, the notion of animals as comfort is part of a cultural tradition and can be traced in Germany's rich heritage of stories and fairy tales. A shortened version of one goes like this:

> Once upon a time there was an old man. He did not bathe, nor did he cook, nor did he leave his house. One day a dog appeared and said: "I am hungry." The man went to the kitchen and cooked him some porridge. When the dog was done, he said: "Clean my fur." The man took a brush and brushed him. When the fur was shiny the dog said: "Walk with me." The man put on his hat and went out with the dog. The dog liked this and stayed with the man and the man enjoyed his life again. (Greiffenhagen and Buck-Werner, 2007, p. 13)

While this is a traditional narrative that sounds like a fairy tale, it is also the beginning of many real-life stories. Animals have a positive effect on people who are open to them and can accomplish in seconds what professional doctors take months to do.

To bring home this point, it is worth pointing out a groundbreaking experiment known as the Parakeet Experiment, which was conducted in thirty-seven nursing homes in England and documented in 1975. One hundred senior citizens received a parakeet. Another hundred senior citizens received a Begonia plant for which they were to care. After eight weeks, those without a parakeet but with the plant recorded that they still felt lonely whereas only 5 percent of those with a parakeet lamented that they were lonely. Not one of the subjects wanted to give their parakeet back. All parakeet owners felt fortunate to have received their bird, claiming that it distracted them from aches and pains and the feeling of loneliness and prompted them to talk and laugh, feel needed, and offered them a chance to give and receive tenderness. Another surprising finding was that a number of participants began to inform themselves about parakeets by studying scholarly literature on parakeet needs, care, and origin. The simple presence of animals broke up mundane routines, motivated curiosity, and functioned as a social lubricant as participants engaged in conversation, sharing experiences, and research findings (Mugford and M'Comisky, 1975).

The senior years present a time of life when people experience increasingly limited mobility and find themselves with less social contact. Even in the presence of other people, senior citizens are not physically touched as much as younger people and are often ignored in conversations. Animals, as we have discussed, do not judge a person based on age and limitations that come with aging, they offer touch, interaction, and a form of friendship, all qualities that can enhance senior citizens' lives, motivating them to enjoy life.

Without stimulation, elderly patients can lose their interest in life and refuse food, making it impossible for them to recover from an ailment. Stories abound which tell of residents in nursing facilities who have been motivated to eat because of the presence of an animal. The authors can attest to being called to sit by a patient with their therapy dog and to encourage eating. Unfortunately, this is not allowed at some nursing homes which require that no dogs be present during mealtimes for hygienic purposes.

Other benefits abound: senior citizens can strengthen hand muscles and improve coordination by touching an animal or holding a leash and ultimately regaining abilities the patients had thought they had lost. Dementia and Alzheimer's sufferers may be reminded of days gone by and begin to recount stories of their past. Patients who have stopped talking altogether, thereby causing their own isolation from human interaction, have been known to talk again.

Other findings have shown that the mere presence of an animal can cause the oft encountered aggression in Alzheimer's patients to subside, leading to more peaceful and effective contact with caretakers. Emotions are stirred in the presence of animals as memories of pets come alive. Past emotions experienced with the pets can be reawakened, sometimes causing sadness at remembering the loss, but often joy as well. These emotions come back to life as the memory is relived.

THE TOUCH OF ANIMALS:
CONTRIBUTIONS FROM BIRTH TO DEATH

Physically, the benefits of touch cannot be underestimated. Petting an animal stirs feelings of connection and ultimately well-being. On the other hand, the absence of touch can result in the opposite. In studies of orphans in Russia, it was found that many were unable to integrate appropriately into society specifically because they had lacked touch in their childhoods. In a study conducted in 2000, Fujimura found that orphans and street children struggled in their ability to form lasting bonds:

> These children often attach very quickly but only briefly to complete strangers. It is as if they cannot get too close. For some it is a fear of impending loss of a relationship once closeness has been established and the heart has been opened. For others, it is the inability to connect on a deeper level. Indeed, how could they, having never experienced closeness as a child? (Fujimura, 2005, p. 79)

At the orphanage, Fujimura was reprimanded by orphanage workers for holding the children. "Don't show them too much affection" they explained, "Once you leave, they may never experience it again and may feel abandoned again" (ibid.). Without even an animal to touch, children in such orphanages are stressed, lack in their sense of personal safety and an ability to empathize (Bryant and Whorley, 1989; Ascione, 1992, pp. 176–191).

Over the course of a human's life, the mere presence of animals, dogs in particular, can further the development of human socialization and learning. In 2002, in Austria, pedagogue Retzlaff took on the project "School with Jule," throughout which a teacher brought his dog, Jule, to school each day for one year. The impact on the students' attitudes toward class and the teacher were significantly altered. Beyond being seen as an authority figure, the teacher was seen as a nurturer and a "human" with strengths and weaknesses. As a result, students, even the most timid, opened up, their concentration levels increased and fewer fights among children ensued. In the end, the children learned more than others in similar classes without dogs (Olbrich and Otterstedt, 2003).

An outcome of this research is the development of animal-assisted reading programs in libraries in the United States. These programs encourage children to read to a nonjudgmental audience and because dogs are usually not allowed in libraries, it becomes a special event for children. Positive associations of reading to a dog enhance children's attitude toward reading in general and of course, by practicing over time, skills improve, making reading even more enjoyable. Many children are motivated by the presence of a dog and will do just about anything to be near one as the following story shows:

> Usually young children participate in these programs however, one day during such a program, in walked a twelve-year-old boy with a 300-page novel to read. I mentioned that we might not finish the book today and he smiled: "I know." he said. "I am not here because I have a hard time reading. I just wanted to spend time with the dog. But I will read if you'd like me to!" (Author's story, 2017)

Furthermore, children who find it hard to socialize benefit from an animal companion as they become noticed, in a positive way, by others. Such children are suddenly viewed by their peers as interesting and approachable. At the same time, children with companion animals develop a sense of responsibility, a deeper understanding of their abilities to contribute to society, and achieve heightened self-confidence as they begin to see themselves as capable actors (Bergesen, 1989).

With the presence of animals, a person can discover a sense of personhood. One gentleman confined to a wheelchair was able, through Animal Assisted Therapy to achieve the optimal relaxed state allowing him to open up truthfully to himself. More specifically, he found that much of his sense of helplessness and frustration stems from the fact that people assume things about him, take control of his body by making decisions for him without seeing him as a capable and thinking individual. It was through therapy that he discovered himself as capable and worthy of respect. He offers his story:

> One morning, for example, I was trying to cross a street. I will confess that I was not at the crosswalk but had in mind to cross the small carless street at another spot. Suddenly a woman grabbed my wheelchair in which I was sitting without even saying hello. After words were had she relayed that she had assumed that I was not only physically disabled but also mentally, simply because I was in a wheelchair. (Friend, 2016)

During therapy sessions, a patient is the center of attention, with his dreams and needs considered by another or others. Animal Assisted Therapy helps patients ponder this concept as they reflect calmly and in quiet, a context rarely met in a life that is punctuated by being pushed and pulled, often unwillingly, physically, in different directions. Animals can help bring the necessary calm for the meditation and concentration necessary to rise above an understanding of self as open to manipulation and force (Olbrich and Otterstedt, 2003, p. 276).

Since the 1980s, hospice has opened its doors to Pet Therapy teams and other forms of therapy to offer a sense of calm, mindfulness, and improve a person's quality of life even when that life is not for long. Some hospices allow the patients to bring their own pet so that they may be together until the time that the patient departs from this world. With an animal at their side they become less anxious as the time approaches, feel a sense of love and being loved, companionship, and a soothing transition on their end-of-life journey.

EFFECTIVENESS OF ANIMAL THERAPY

Theoretical explanations for the effectiveness of animal therapy are to date vague and incomplete. The majority of explanations stem from research on human interactions with companion animals. Unfortunately, these studies have not been sufficiently extended to include interactions between therapist, patient, and animal in therapeutic situations. We are still taking baby steps to increase our understanding, especially as the concept of introducing animals into therapy sessions is also only beginning to gain acceptance.

There is no singular comprehensive and conclusive scholarly theory on the variety of ways in which and why Animal Assisted Therapy is successful. Many studies have been conducted that point to aspects of its success. However, that animals contribute significantly to human well-being cannot be denied. To summarize then, here is what we do know:

- Certain animals automatically speak to the emotional lives of individuals, help them open up and thereby ease the therapist's ability to interact with the patient.
- Because chronically ill patients and elderly patients in particular may feel a lack of human contact, physical and emotional, animals can prove critical for their sense of well-being.
- Animals are specialists in nonverbal communication and great interpreters of body language. Thus, they are able to communicate with patients who suffer from communicative delays or challenges, such as children struggling with autism. Animals help build bridges between therapist and client.
- Caring for an animal enriches people's lives by helping to structure the daily activities and giving people a sense of responsibility and personal value.
- For people suffering with memory loss, an animal can help to bring back childhood or other memories which can elicit speech from formerly silent patients.
- Touch and tenderness in and of itself makes people feel good but also helps the development of babies and children, motivates people to feel accepted and loved, and eases anxiety (Hart in Fine, 2010, pp.59–84).
- Animals motivate patients to engage in therapy and to be open to new therapeutic methods.
- Therapy animals can reduce stress and even function as rewards. They ease a patient's transition to new levels of therapy and offer a sense of security and emotional support. Through such support, patients are capable of adapting and changing their learned response model to a new one. This is especially the case in working with patients suffering from phobias, depression, post-traumatic stress syndrome, and others.

Careful preparation and training for animals engaged in such therapy is important. During our research we found out that, for example, therapy dogs are trained to respond at the appropriate moment to specific emotional states of humans. They learn when to approach a fearful child and how to assume bodily contact. They can learn how to mitigate anger responses in patients and how to comfort them, noting minimal hand gestures and voice signals. Better than humans, animals can learn to pick up on the slightest emotional states and changes and help balance, motivate, or excite, as necessary. They do so without overwhelming the patient and independently, without the help of the human therapist.

Still, more research needs to be done to support assessment on an individual basis of patients, given that not all will necessarily benefit the same way from Pet Therapy. This can be dependent on whether or not a patient is raised with pets. Someone growing up with dogs, for example, might find a dog comforting and yet, it not being her own pet, might cause her to be less open to a new animal. Further research on the impact of prior experiences with pets on individual personality traits is thus necessary. Even less clear is which species of animals are best suited for which therapy; for example, which animals are able to communicate best with humans, which possess the right temperament to answer different emotional needs, and even which size animal is best suited for certain therapy sessions (Hart, 2000).

PROTECTION OF SERVICE AND THERAPY DOGS

Finally, we would like to address one last topic: that of the protection of animals in Animal Assisted and Pet Therapy. Unfortunately, there is no law that ensures the well-being of animals as they are used to further human well-being. While in many countries in Europe and in the United States attempts are made to alleviate animal cruelty, in many other regions of the world there are no similar laws.

Animal cruelty laws in the United States and Europe are comprehensive, however, they merely offer guidelines on limits that under no circumstances are to be crossed and if crossed will lead to legal consequences. However, limitations are fuzzy at times. Let us take, for example, the case of a service dog, trained to stand at the side of her human day and night unless told otherwise. She can help to carry and bring objects, open doors, help a person get dressed, and lead her person through traffic, offer a signal to alert for illness or seizures, to mention only a few possibilities. We have here a situation of a canine worker who is on the job 24/7. Of course, no dog is a machine and thus requires exercise, play, and free time to decompress and to be a dog. Playing with other dogs would certainly enhance a service dog's well-being too. Society, its infrastructure and rules surrounding service animals, neglect the fact that an animal is more like a human than a tool, similarly requiring leisure time to perform effectively. After years of animal training and behavior modification, Nommensen found that people requiring service dogs may not have the ability to offer off-leash opportunities for the dog and may worry about loss of control of their canine worker and companion. Spaces where dogs can run freely are limited as well and few recreation areas offer access to wheelchairs. Increasing wheelchair access and access to people with disabilities in general is an aspect many societies are seeking to develop, but few would think to include dog areas as part of the agenda. Nor do we think of the importance of such defined times and spaces for all working dogs as, for example, search and rescue dogs and police dogs. Working animals, especially therapy animals, run the risk of overexertion: "My dogs need a lot of down time between therapy sessions . . . I need to be vigilant and not see too many patients in one day" (Hahn, interview, 2017).

Sometimes Hahn is forced to cancel appointments as the day evolves into one that requires more energy from her dogs than expected. "Every day is different," Hahn adds, "and so I must make decisions in the middle of a planned day on how best to serve both my dogs and my patients" (Hahn, interview, 2017).

Nommensen and Fujimura found similar comments throughout their interviews with therapists and volunteer teams in medical facilities. In yet another interview with a therapist serving suicide-prone patients, Nommensen discovered the importance of distinguishing between work and free time for animal-therapists. One therapist utilizes a harness which she puts on Leo, a Labrador Retriever, which indicates to him when to indicate that a patient is suicidal. When the harness is off, he knows he is not working. Since Leo often visits patients in school settings, using his harness as a signal is not as obvious and does not cause stress among students. As a result of ethnographic research conducted specifically for this book, the importance of proper care of the animal-therapist is of essence for effective treatment of patients.

Moreover, the relationship between handler and animal-therapist is significant. Those interviewed found that their relationship to their working animals is more like the one a person can have to a colleague and the word "partnership" was frequently used. All human-animal therapy teams described their partnership as "very close" and emphasized the importance of careful and caring daily interactions with their animals in order to meet the needs of both animal and patient: "The talents possessed by the animal-therapist are unique—so it is obvious that I not simply use my animals as an instrument in my work—but as living beings with special needs, which I gladly meet as they enrich my work as human therapist!" (Hahn, interview, 2017).

Today the service of animals to enhance our well-being is recognized as extremely valuable in the lives of humans who enjoy their company. It must be emphasized however, that their help is only possible in the context of a culture that elevates animals above other non-human life and material forms such as plants and objects and further accepts them as positive creatures. In the West, we recognize animals as similar to us, as harboring a personality and to some even a soul. As we move on to explore the cultural ramifications of the potential for animals to enhance human well-being, we end with a quote from a popular German forester, Peter Wohlleben, who is also an expert on the subject of the emotional lives of animals. His insights confirm what we may have surmised, that animals are emotionally similar to us:

> I enjoy looking for analogies between animals and humans, because I cannot imagine that they feel differently. The possibility, that I am correct in this belief is quite high. . . . To be sure, our senses can mislead us to read too much into the behaviors of dogs and cats. But the majority of the time our intuition is

correct—I am certain of that. Current scientific findings (of the complexity of animal feelings) come as no surprise to animal lovers, rather, they simply confirm that we can trust our interpretations of how animals feel. (Wohlleben, 2016, pp. 225–228)

CONCLUSION

This chapter set out to offer a glance at the complex history of the use of animals in therapy. As we have seen, the magnitude of opportunities to use animals in therapy is growing, be it to support and develop human fine motor skills, physical and psychological rehabilitation, speech therapy, or in emotional and psychological therapy sessions to treat phobias, attention-deficit/hyperactivity disorder, and more. This form of therapy is especially useful in treating patients who do not respond positively to conventional settings or in cases of outpatient care. Because of the positive responses to such Animal Assisted Therapies, it is time to integrate it into more common praxis, rather than keeping it as a marginalized and alternative method. For such general use to take effect, more research needs to be done, as described above. Findings of neurological benefits are often incomplete. Also, long-term benefits are rarely discussed. Rather, we have focused on immediate responses of the patient to Animal Assisted Therapy but have not followed such patients beyond therapy. However, we cannot stress enough that the findings we do possess thus far are extremely hopeful, given in reports by patients looking back on their experiences. Nommensen and Fujimura agree that continuing research on outcomes of Animal Assisted Therapy will only benefit the progress of patient recovery in a variety of medical contexts.

Questions that remain to be answered include to what extent can studies be conducted that focus on specific health, mental or physical, issues in a variety of cultural and personal contexts. Positive results could lead to programs that would allow patients to search for the appropriate animal therapies available to them. Another issue that needs to be resolved is the cultural acknowledgment of human-animal therapy teams as a valid profession with appropriate and standardized education, training, and assessment.

Once a society has come to accepting the benefit of animals to human well-being, has acknowledged a professional space in its society for such work, and has developed educational systems, continuing education in the field is equally important, as new findings come in from contemporary research and to enable effective up-to-date treatment. Such educational concepts have been designed and proposed for wider use by organizations in Switzerland (Therapy Dogs of Switzerland, VTHS), Austria (European Society for Animal Assisted Therapy, ESAAT) and the United States (Pet Partners, formerly Delta Organization). These programs have not been recognized on a state-wide level even though countries such as the United States and a number in the European Union offer quality education with bachelor degrees and professional certification.[4] These established programs compete with numerous less qualified programs that are advertised by individuals frequently lacking education in training and certification. Ultimately, societal acceptance, government recognition, as well as medical sanctioning of educational programs and professionalization of human-animal therapy teams is essential for quality control and progress of Animal Assisted Therapy and positive human-animal interactions enabling mutual well-being.

NOTES

1. http://www.historyofyork.uk/themes/georgian/the-retreat. Accessed August 31, 2016.
2. http://www.greenchimneys.org. Accessed January 12, 2016.
3. http://www.hestura.de. Accessed January 17, 2017.
4. http://www.esaat.org and http://www.animaledu.com. Accessed May 1, 2017.

Chapter Two

Cultural Foundations of Human-Animal Relations

As we have shown in previous chapters, interacting with animals is acknowledged in various social contexts as offering a sense of physical and psychological well-being and contributing to making lives more meaningful. While we tend to see our relationships with animals as one of mutual benefit both in companionship and in therapy situations, one in which we offer love and tenderness as the pets offer support and empathy, ironically, the idea of animals as promoters of human well-being is founded on an understanding of human dominion over animals rather than an equality in the human-animal relationship. As a result, while the well-being of humans may be furthered in various societies, that of animals may be neglected.

In order to better understand how certain societies have learned to view animals as benefitting the human experience, this chapter explores beliefs surrounding animals as working and nonworking members of human society that are grounded in culturally specific traditions and worldviews. We will begin with discussing the significance of culture in understanding human-animal interactions, that is, the language and behaviors people use to exhibit their relationships to pets as grounded in historical belief systems. Representations of our interactions with pets and nature emanate from cultural values, some of which can be traced to belief systems. While we find many similarities cross-culturally, particularities exist between regions of the world.

Both via a review of the literature and ethnographic research, Fujimura explores changes in attitudes toward animals in Germany, Japan, Russia, and the United States. The chapter then moves on to discuss how the concept of dominion over animals is grounded in world religions. Japan and Russia represent interesting case studies given their unique histories, each with deep connections to spirituality and religion and more recent developments in utilizing animals for service and therapy.

Japan, in particular, presents an interesting case with complex spiritual roots in Shintoism and Buddhism. Historically, these religions conflicted with European and U.S. imperial and colonial dominion. As religion informs social attitudes and perceptions of nature, Japanese attitudes toward animal keeping contrasted with those of Europe and the United States. According to Skabelund (2011), European industrial progress of the late nineteenth century, including notions of dog keeping and breeding, were part of European cultural hegemony (p. 4). Skabelund refers to this link between imperialism and companion animals "canine imperialism" (p. 2). Certainly, other countries could offer similar yet equally distinct examples of diverse foundations for the integration of animals, in particular dogs, into society and so this chapter functions as a stepping stone for future cultural studies.

For the collection of documentation of the development of attitudes toward human interaction with and keeping of companion animals, we begin with an overview of Buddhism in Japan as documented in art and scholarly historical literature and how these belief systems struggled with changing attitudes toward animals as imported belief systems from European countries. We end our look at Japan with a glimpse at the rapidly developing uses of animals for education, comfort, and companionship as discovered via interviews and current scholarship.

Russia offers a cultural history that developed out of ancient Slavic beliefs and later Russian Orthodoxy. The ancient traditions included beliefs in spirits of nature, such as forest and tree spirits, as well as Russian pagan divinities. Some of these beliefs continued even with the introduction of Russian Orthodoxy. Russian spirituality is an integration of both its own Orthodoxy and pagan beliefs that emphasizes connections to animals and plants and is expressed throughout Russian literature. Thus, as we venture to study Russia, we begin with an overview of the literature that focuses on the development of cultural attitudes toward animals. We end with a discussion of contemporary Russian attitudes toward interactions with animals, both as companions and as therapists. While the initial discussion is based on her literature, a cherished treasure of Russia, we end with insights based on participant-observation research and interviews.

With this chapter, the authors hope to introduce the concept of the significance of cultural studies to better understand why people treat animals the way they do, that our treatment is not simply on a whim, but deeply embedded in beliefs, traditions, and symbolism, which cannot be denied when interacting with other societies, their people, their medical institutions, and their social and government organizations. After all, each culture's history must be respected in order to effectively communicate with one another.

THE IMPORTANCE OF CULTURE

Let us begin with a look at the tip of the cultural iceberg: the most visible, audible, or obvious-to-the-outsider ways in which people communicate relationships. These would include language, cultural artifacts such as art, common practices, and religious texts. People interact with others, including animals, by negotiating relationships through manipulation of the self and others and often through outright control (Mitchell in Pregowski, 2016, p. viii). This process is reflected in cultural narratives, including social norms and religious texts that guide our daily lives. Thus, we find dominion reinforced in cultural and spiritual rituals and habits which further transmit and reflect unspoken values concerning our attitudes toward animals. How we speak of and to animals, for example, calling them "good boy" or when we name them traditional dog names like "Lassie" or even non-names like "Buttercup" or "Peanut," albeit endearing, reinforces their lesser status in our society. It is via the names we give our companion animals that we communicate what they represent to us (Pregowski, 2016, p. 236), be it a gadget (as in the name Gizmo), a friend (as in the name Buddy) or a family member (any nickname or Baby), symbolic of a value (Lucky, for example), or other metaphoric names. Expressions of power through habits or ritualized behavior that assert our control over the animal (training a dog to shake or play dead) is normalized in daily life. While some of these behaviors are necessary for living with a companion animal (training it to go outside or sit rather than jump all over us), others are simply at our own whim and amusement (sitting up, jumping through hoops). In short, how we interact with the companion animals, the language we assign to them and use to describe them, the tradition of training them, varyingly in diverse contexts, both influence and symbolize how we think about them. Underlying values determining our relationship with animals and specifically our often-subconscious belief in animals as contributors to human well-being in specific societies can be understood by studying people's culturally unique interactions with their animals and the language surrounding these interactions.

In complex societies such as those in Asia, Europe, and the United States, the cultural value placed on dominion over pets extends to the belief in certain animals as human property. As living beings, animals are valued for their ability to serve and respond to human expectations. These expectations, in turn, are based on our assumptions of the essence of our pets. Popular animal trainers will preface their work with their basic beliefs about the nature of specific animals, such as dogs, in order to direct people how best to interact with them. As we write, there is a trend in the culture of dog training enthusiasts and behaviorists, especially in Germany but increasingly in the United States, to respect dogs for who they are, to learn to adapt to their language rather than to assume we can easily impose our own. Whereas in the late nineteenth and early twentieth centuries animals were expected to discover our needs and expectations and respond to our verbal commands with little regard for their own needs and natural ways of expressing these. Today many trainers emphasize taking the animal's uniqueness and ability to feel, think, and behave in ways that should be respected.

Norwegian dog trainer and behaviorist Rugaas has garnered a large following of trainers who espouse the importance of reading what dogs tell us through signals they send us in order to build a relationship with the dog prior to shaping their behavior as opposed to forcing behavior. In her research, Rugaas has discovered that dogs are continuously communicating with us in ways that are often hidden from plain human sight or misinterpreted. According to Rugaas, "Dogs use signals as soon as there is anything to calm down. If they are awake, they "talk," just like you and I . . . Other dogs see (their signals), even other animals, like cats. All it takes is a little practice and knowing what to look for" (Rugaas, 2006, p. 4). Because of her work, a subculture of dog trainers has emerged that focuses on a secret language we need to decipher as humans in order to effectively and humanely work with dogs.

Students that follow methods unique to their trainer can in some cases form subcultures wherein the followers form an integrated network of working with their animals, beliefs about their relationship with them, and attitudes toward themselves in relation to their pets. The United States harbors many such trainers around whom followers have gathered, often in opposition to other methodologies. These subcultures have been able to flourish, especially with the help of social media, establishing networks nationwide. In the Washington, DC, and Baltimore region in the United States, for example, one trainer, Hartwell, has reached a guru-like standing to his followers to the point that his followers have learned a special language to speak with their dogs. In contrast to those trainers who see dogs more akin to humans in emotions, Hartwell takes as his premise for training that dogs are unlike humans. They are dogs first and only with an understanding of natural canine behavior can shaping specific desirable behaviors begin. After all, many of the behaviors we expect of our canine companions, such as agility, freestyle, or certain movement patterns in obedience and rally, do not come naturally to them. Because of his record of rehabilitating aggressive dogs, Hartwell has established a name for himself, to the point that his followers may recognize each other as part of his tribe, encountering each other as they make use of Hartwell's training commands, commands that are derived from the Japanese words. Members of the subculture find pride in their common beliefs about dogs and, according to one member, "we know better so our dogs do better. It's hard not to want to try to preach to every dog owner I know how to do it 'right'" (Micah, 2016).

Hartwell's philosophy begins with the idea that a dog has dog "essence," a combination of wolf origin and breeding, the latter resulting in a desire of dogs to serve humans. It is the human's job to develop this essence and potential while simultaneously protecting and ensuring the companion animal's well-being. In effect, according to Hartwell, we must honor the concept of dominion of animals and all that the concept of dominion implies. At the heart of his training philosophy, much as with others' like Rugaas, is that we need to recognize the dog as a dog first (Millan, 2006). We are witnessing a shift in the United States and Europe from completely dominating animals to working with them as partners.

Caesar Millan has cultivated an international following which values his unique way of handling dogs. In his seminars, Millan emphasizes his view of dogs and how they must be understood before training can begin: "First I see a dog as an animal, then species, then the breed, then the name" (Millan, 2016). According to him as well as the above-mentioned trainers and behaviorists (and many others), anthropomorphizing is what causes most problems with companion animals in households. The tendency in some societies to idealize animals as the perfect companion, superior to a human companion in some cases, which complicates interspecies relations. "By not being able to speak our language, and thus, not being able to judge or criticize us, companion animals are, in a way, 'ideal humans,' at least until they display their animal nature, for example, when they pee on the carpet" (as cited in Pregowski, 2016).

In Western Europe, the owner-pet model reflects a philosophical worldview of approaching others in an "us-them" or "othering" manner, whereby the other is seen as occupying a different social identity, and because of the difference, an assumed inferior one. The pet then is at the mercy of the owner, socially constructed not simply as a non-human animal, but as a pet, a term originating in the sixteenth century and referring to a kept animal and indulged child (see Merriam-Webster online dictionary) and thus, not an equal adult. The us-them dichotomy leads to the idea of "otherness" which in the social sciences is a category through which we can study the construction of majority, minority, and marginalized identities as well as relationships of equality, servitude, and dominion.

DOMINION OVER COMPANION ANIMALS
IN WORLD RELIGIONS

Both in the United States and many European countries, nations whose ideologies are to an extent founded on Christian teachings, dominion of animals has been historically presumed. To illuminate this underlying belief, we can turn to religious and folk narratives. Dominion, as expressed in religious texts, for example, implies a set of moral obligations. According to such narratives, beyond keeping animals as workers and pets, dominion implies that it is a person's responsibility to ensure that his or her animals experience minimal harm, pain, stress, and suffering. This obligation is found in many religions including Islam, Hinduism, Buddhism, and Christianity. According to these religions, animals are more than simply kept, but should be respected. In Islam, for example, humans, the servants of Allah, must ensure that no harm comes to animals, unless there is a need. Any unnecessary ill treatment of animals is a sin (Szűcs et al., 2012, p. 1503). Hinduism, by comparison, considers everybody a capsule capable of holding spirits. To protect the spirits and to help them on the path to reincarnation, the code of sarva-bhuta-hita (Szűcs et al., 2012, p. 1502) requires that people show devotion to all living beings.

A more extreme approach, which offers complete deference to animals, may be found in Jainism, an ancient religion in India which specifically focuses on nonviolence toward all living beings as the main path to liberation of the soul. This form of nonviolence is a practice called Ahisma, the essence of Jainism. As all living beings are considered to have divine potential, any harm or intervention in a living being's life will affect the balance of the universe and any violence toward living beings including oneself is taboo. Jains work each day to ensure not only continued life, but well-being of all animals and plants.

Jainists and Buddhists agree that all living beings are motivated to live. Unlike Buddhists, however, Jainists believe that all creatures are equivalent because they all contain an equal essence. Thus, Jains take extensive measures to ensure that they as individuals cause no harm. Examples include discouraging walking outdoors when it is dark as one might step on an insect and wearing gauze masks to avoid accidentally swallowing them (Szűcs et al., 2012).

Buddhism respects life in all its forms and advocates that humans in no way harm or hinder animals to live a full life. Keeping animals for companionship is seen as threatening an animal's welfare. The concern among Buddhists that the use of pets as companions hurts animals, is not to be underestimated. In the West, the owner-pet model of human-animal relations is one that is seen by Buddhists as perpetuating the victimization of animals. Until recently, Western societies paid little heed to the true effects on the animal, and, according to Buddhists, have debased the spirit of the animal.

Throughout many religions there is a fundamental tenet which ranks any non-human animal as lower. For Buddhists, being human is considered a moral achievement, and therefore, because non-human animals cannot aspire to the same morality and intellect, some Buddhists argue that humans are "entitled to benefit from practices that (are) obviously harmful to some other animals" (Waldau, 2002, p. 6). Depending on the Buddhist denomination the role of animals in society varies. Buddhism has many different iterations and so, for example, a Buddhist in Thailand is very different from a Buddhist in modern-day Japan. To make matters even more complex, attitudes toward animals are developed in a constant dynamic of religion and society adapting to each other's changes, resulting in the use of and care for animals being in constant flux.

We turn now to an overview of beliefs toward companion animals as healers in Japan and Russia. Attitudes in both countries are discussed as outcomes of belief systems, evidenced in art and literature. A glance at art and aesthetics in Japan and an overview of literary representations of animals in Russia frame the ethnographic findings in this chapter.

Japan

As in other parts of the world, pets in Japan were originally a commodity largely for elites. Being able to surround oneself or keep animals continues to be a luxury as animals have historically inspired spirituality, emotional balance, comfort, and even playfulness, values deemed as answering higher needs above food and shelter. Animals in Japan are believed to be kin to humans, and beyond kinship in Buddhism and Shinto religions, and are endowed at times with divinity. Their exoticism and beauty symbolize and awaken in us a sense of the essence of life and a respect for the natural world. Such feelings about animals are depicted in early Japanese art (Nature, Pleasure, Myth Animals in the Art of Japan, Amherst Gallery Exhibit), where animals are painted on various materials to convey messages and beliefs. Some of these artistic representations were used to educate and entertain both adults and children on the subjects of Buddhism, the zodiac signs, or social parables. Other times they facilitated government messages as in prints used to reinvent historical and mythical subjects in order to maintain and revitalize government control. Such depictions and messages can be found especially in the art of the Edo period which impressed upon the viewer "the quality of the Edo culture at a time of sociopolitical uncertainty in Japan (Animals in the Art of Japan, Amherst Gallery Exhibit).

Even though Buddhists do not traditionally support confinement of animals as it is seen to limit an animal's freedom and natural life, Buddhist clergy have found it necessary to soften this perspective. Companion animals have become increasingly popular in modern Japan, so much so that Buddhist practices now include animals in familial life-cycle rituals. Historically animals were largely kept in Japan for aesthetic purposes and thus included mainly animals considered to be beautiful such as exotic birds, fish, purebred cats, and lapdogs ("chin"). With the rise of the middle class, more breeds were imported as pets symbolized the material wherewithal for a family to provide beyond the basics. Pets represented luxuries that helped to define the

American modern middle-class lifestyle (Skabelund, 2011, p. 173). Slowly but surely, the concept of the pet as a material luxury item, ornament as well as companion, developed (p. 173).

As animals began living in Japanese households, the way in which they were referred to also changed. Indeed, the inclusion of animals as pets can be traced linguistically. Tracing how societies change their terminology helps to uncover a society's orientations, perspectives, and tensions, however, language does not reflect a straightforward process of society and history. The development of language can at once include the invention of new terminology, alteration of older terminology and transfer of terms to incorporate new meanings. Language develops in ways that represent social dynamics: "such changes are not always either simple or final. Earlier and later senses coexist, or become actual alternatives in which problems of contemporary belief and affiliation are contested" (p. 22).

The way in which we refer to our surroundings influences, and is influenced by, internal dynamics and cross-cultural pollination.

We can trace attitudes toward pets by following linguistic transformations in terminology referring to them. Among the traditional upper class, pets in Japan were acquired for pleasure and were referred to as "aigan dobutstu," meaning toy animal and expressing the attitude toward pets as possessions and play things. Today, the integration of companion animals into family life makes this term no longer popular. Instead, "katei dobutsu," family animal, is more appropriate in contemporary Japan (Ambros, 2012).

As in many other countries, in Japan, pets are at times included in and assigned a distinct family role. One mother and naval officer's wife, Maeyama-san (2017) tells her reason for purchasing a dog:

> When we moved back to our home town, we were back in our own house with a garden. Haruna, our daughter was now in elementary school and, because she has no sisters or brothers, we thought it would be good for her to grow up with a dog so she can have a playmate, like a sister or brother. Also, she would learn to care for another being and train too. (Interview with Maeyama-san, January 2017)

Maeyama-Sensei, her husband, a professor and commander in the navy expands:

> We also feel it is important for Haruna to understand the full life circle. A dog does not live as long as a human so we will experience all facets of life, from puppyhood through adulthood, sickness and ultimately death. It is important for Haruna to learn about all these aspects as she grows up. Including death. But also, how to treat family members and for her, of course, the dog is also a sibling. (Interview with Maeyama-Sensei, 2017)

As a new sibling and teacher of life lessons, their dog needed to be taught to live in a human family and adapt to human ways, in a brother-like way. What would this mean? Most important to the Maeyama family was that the dog be friendly, playful, and teachable. They bought a dog, a Corgi, from a pet store because, as she says, both Maeyama-san's husband and daughter fell in love with him. Unfortunately, training a dog is only beginning to become a practice in Japan, with most Japanese trainers coming from the field of police dog training. While Maeyama-san read books she found in the library that focused on police training and discipline and some of which used positive reinforcement, it was easier at times to raise the dog as she might a child. Maeyama-san explains:

> Japanese people are not so serious about training dogs like in the United States. But in the past few years, I can see Japanese interest in dog training growing as internet sites and TV programs are growing in number.
>
> Six years ago (2011) when I bought Randy, our Corgi, there was not so much information, so I borrowed old training books including some by Makoto Morita and Satoshi Fujii from the library. They are both police dog trainers, each with different methods. I prefer Fujii's method which focuses on the dog holding still, muzzle control and the gentle lead walking. The books helped but he still barks a lot. I suppose I do not train enough as he is first and foremost a family member and after all, we educate, not train, family members. (Interview with Maeyama-san, January 2017)

Different cultures have different child rearing methods. In Japan, children at a young age are given freedom to explore. It is not until they enter school that discipline enters the education process. Maeyama-san's dog did receive initial discipline, but the continuation of training has lessened as the dog continues to be the child in the family and, according to her experience growing up, babies and small children need to have experiences on their own terms, freely explore and enjoy life first, then learn.

As animals went from "play things" to family members, the institution of Buddhism in Japan recognized the significance of animals in people's lives and adapted to changing social customs of including pets in households. Rather than decry the keeping of animals, today they are included in Buddhist mortuary rites of passage for the deceased. Some have criticized this practice as opportunistic, as a reaction to Buddhism losing traction in modern Japanese society.

> In late modernity, as the ties between parish temples and parishioners had begun to erode with changing demographics, urbanization, and the development of a secular funeral industry, Buddhist temples have sought new ways in which to capitalize on their expertise in mortuary rites. Extending such rituals to mizuko, nonhuman beneficiaries has been one way to increase revenue for

the temple while claiming continued relevance in their patron's lives. (Ambros, 2012, p. 7)

Traditional Buddhism is losing ground in an increasingly secular Japan, so allowing society to influence ritual changes may be one way of keeping Buddhism relevant.

Small living quarters and an all-consuming work ethic in Japan make it difficult for people to keep a pet. With the realization of the benefits of companion animals in Japan, businesses have opened access to pets, and are thriving. Pet cafés with various animal attractions have become fashionable as of late, offering cats, rabbits, birds, goldfish, goats, and penguins with whom one might enjoy a cup of tea. A goldfish, Kingyozaka in Tokyo, goes back 350 years and is a place where people can have tea, view and buy goldfish. Other cafés became popular following the opening of the first cat café in Osaka, 2004.

Each café has its own allure, from allowing people to view, to cuddle, even to walk the animals depending on the species and café's rules. In one Tokyo café clients may walk rabbits while another allows the walking of its goats. Bird cafés and reptile cafés, on the other hand, tend to permit viewing only, although some will let a person pet a reptile or bring their own bird.

Cafés such as these are populated by customers for varying reasons. Neko (cat) cafés in particular have been noted for helping clients' distress and/or in helping them establish human relationships: functioning as "a social lubricant facilitating conversation" (Niijima, 2016, p. 275). One computer specialist from Tokyo expressed his reasons:

> When work is very stressful, I go for tea. With the tea and the cats, I am warmed inside and out. I feel balanced and at ease. As a man, I worry my colleagues will see me, but so far that has not happened. I need it to calm me down. (Interview with Maeyama-san, 2016)

The therapeutic value of animals is catching on in Japan too, beginning at the café level and extending to official training of animals to visit hospitals and senior care programs.

Social stresses cause people to turn to animals in order to facilitate communication. Animals of various species, while appreciated for their charms and benefits in countries such as Japan, are becoming commodities to be utilized for the well-being of both individual and society. They contribute not only to well-being of consumers, but, in a society with low economic growth, also promote socioeconomic transformations with new professions in the management and keeping of such growing animal industries. Well-being for individuals includes not only emotional and social stability or other medical definitions, but the ability to thrive economically as well. These businesses are spreading globally with pet cafés germinating in Australia, Europe, and

North America (p. 279). Similar pet cafés in the United States are being established to help find homes for homeless pets, as the coffee business in the United States offers a better lure to viewing such animals as does a shelter.

Russia

Russia's cultural views and values are well represented in her oral and literary traditions, which in turn are based on a complex religious system, a combination of Orthodoxy and pagan beliefs. Much of what is believed and integrated into Russia's modern ideology, including ideas about human identity, relationships between nature and society, as well as healing methods, is traceable to Russia's ethnic roots. It is precisely because of her significant and vibrant oral and later literary tradition, that we look at Russia's perspective via a discussion of narratives, some of which invoke what it means to be Russian, what it means to be human, and the special place assigned to certain animals in Russian society. Russian "pet" keeping and attitudes toward domestic animals in particular can be studied by looking at Russia's vast literary tradition.

Animals, and specifically dogs, are depicted in Russian mythology as a vehicle for humans to access the spirit world beyond the tangible one in which we dwell. A dog's ability to lie between one world and another is due to his constant interaction with humans and their spaces while maintaining close proximity to nature: "There is much of man in his dogs, much of the dog in us, and behind this, much of the wolf in both the dog and man. And, there is some of the Dog-Man in god" (Mondry, 2015, p. 10). Because of their closeness to both nature and society, the often inexplicable and the rational, they are depicted in Russian literature as closer to the spiritual world and, by extension, considered potential help for humans to connect with nature and the spiritual world. It is for this reason that dogs were used as sacrificial animals (Mondry, 2015, p. 11). The powers dogs possess are visible throughout Russian history and led to mixed feelings toward them: on the one hand dogs were cherished for their ability to help humans achieve a better life, on the other they had supernatural powers that could complicate the human experience. It was not until the ninteenth century that a new, less suspicious attitude toward dogs was cultivated, largely due to the influence of Western Europe in particular on Russia's middle class (Mondry, 2015).

Dogs can be viewed as vulnerable precisely because of their supernatural powers that also open their souls to otherworldly forces, good or evil. They can both exert their power to affect human life, but may be moved by other forces as they act as vessels for spirits of the deceased. Absent such forces however, they are a blank slate. Like children, dogs are seen as untainted by adult society and deserving of human protection from evil contexts and potentially harmful spaces. Canine companions are likely to be victims to the whims of people, alive or dead, and so it makes sense to shield them from being cursed or controlled by evil spirits. As one Russian woman describes while preparing a grave for a deceased relative: children and dogs have no business in such places as, for example, graveyards "because souls of the murdered get into them" (Pesmen, 2000, p. 113). Dogs are seen as innocent and easily manipulated by the more powerful spirits that may dwell in specific spaces because they welcome the human soul.

In nineteenth- and twentieth-century Russian literature, we see dogs' depictions changing from supernatural and fearsome, to beings deserving human empathy and help, especially as they suffer victimization by socioeconomic circumstances, much like humans do throughout Russian history (Pesmen, 2000, p. 117). Turgenev, a famous Russian writer of the nineteenth century wrote: "We (my dog and I) are the same; in each of us there burns and shines the same trembling spark" (Pesmen, 2000, p. xviv). By equating himself to a dog, to possessing a human spark, Turgenev alludes to the belief that dogs, much like humans, possess a soul.

The concept of the soul is a significant key concept that is particularly important to and revealing of Russian culture. Certain Russian words like sud'ba (fate) and dusha (soul) play a particularly important role in Russian culture and offer invaluable insight into the beliefs and motivations of Russians:

> A key word such as dusha . . . in Russian is like one loose end which we have managed to find in a tangled ball of wool: by pulling it, we may be able to unravel a whole tangled "ball" of attitudes, values, and expectations, embodied not only in words, but also in common collocations, in set phrases, in grammatical constructions, in proverbs, and so on. (Wierzbicka, 1997, p. 16–17)

Poems, stories, and entire books have been written to explain the word "dusha." Having "dusha" is a uniquely human experience. To Russians, dusha is the essence of people, a life force that relates to "compassion and suffering" and has even been described as a form of Russian national character (Pesmen, 2000, p. 4). Russians are proud of embodying a particular soul, deeply connected with the larger Russian soul, a Russian experience, one that has suffered but must persevere.

To Russians, dogs, unlike most other animals,[1] mirror humans and are depicted in literature as having types of souls as well: wise, powerful, gentle, or other. To many, and especially to those working with dogs at their side, a dog stands above other animals specifically because she or he, like a human, has a soul of its own. One Russian explained: "Any peasant would say his dog is a living dusha" (Pesmen, 2000, p. 156). Because of its soul, a dog is seen to have emotions, feelings, and possibly an afterlife, much like humans.

When Turgenev alludes to a dog as having a soul he brings meaning and prestige to the dog in society.

In the twentieth and twenty-first centuries, the special bond shared by Russian humans and their dogs continues to be represented in literature. Numerous classic and popular works demonstrate that dogs indeed serve as emotional strongholds thereby helping humans cope with society and the hardships of human life. Dogs are described as friends, offering companionship and contributing to the psychological health of those who need them. Russians find comfort in their dogs because dogs are not just sentient beings but subjective, emotional individuals with souls capable of providing real support. Mondry points out in her analysis of Zamyatin's "The Land Surveyor," for example, that as long as humans have emotional needs, dogs are easily employable: "the automaton-like people behind Zamyatin's green wall no longer need animals as friends because they no longer have emotional needs" (Mondry, 2015, p. 187).

Yet, while Russians cherish their pets and utilize them to enhance human well-being, some pets are considered superior for the job. In fact, within a species, some breeds are considered better than others and those with no distinct breed, mixed-breeds, may not be cherished at all. As we turn to contemporary Russia, this nuanced form of speciesism, a bias against a genetic strain within a species which we will call "breedism," becomes even more pronounced.

Upon arrival in Russia in 2001 with my family which included my husband, two toddlers and two dogs, I immediately sought out a dog-walker to help with the daily routine. We had come to Moscow as a diplomatic family while I was on sabbatical to conduct ethnographic research. I had been forewarned that many people previously hired to work for diplomatic families such as nannies, cooks and drivers and yes, dog-walkers were simultaneously employed by the FSB (formerly known as KGB, our CIA equivalent). I was also told harrowing stories of poisonings of pets by these employees in order to scare away our CIA. Interviews were thus nothing to be sneezed at and, as a speaker of Russian, I felt I could weed out those who did not empathize with animals. At the very least, I hoped to hire a person who would treat my dogs well while I was out. The fear of hiring a dog-walker who might hurt my dogs was real and yet I believed possible as I was not there to spy. My problem with hiring someone who could "love my dogs like I do" turned out to be very different, yet still problematic.

There was a tendency, I noticed, for the interviewee to look surprised when I showed them my dogs: two mixed breeds—one a shepherd mix, Kopek, that looked more like a dingo that I had rescued from the streets of Chicago and a Dalmatian-mix, Sally. Trying to put on a good face, the interviewees, like my Russian acquaintances, would gravitate toward Sally and only awkwardly pet Kopek. Later my hired dog-walker and friends would confide in me: "It's just that Kopek looks like our street dogs. Not a dog you would have as a pet, put a leash on and walk through town. Not a pure-bred dog" (Moscow 2001). Ultimately the dog-walker would avoid walking on streets and chose instead to go mushroom and berry picking in the woods where no-one would see them. Granted, mushroom and berry picking is an important tradition for many Russians in the summer and I am pretty sure my dogs preferred this to any city hikes, so it all worked out. To be noted however, the ranking of mammals is more subtle than simply ranking one species over another, inter-species, but extends to ranking within a species, that is, intra-species. A kind of racism or, as I noted above, breedism. The street-dog "dvorniashka" is the least favorable in the ranking of dog as pet, to some even unimaginable as such. (Fujimura 2016)

The dvorniashka, while on the one hand not considered good for social well-being, is, on the other hand, admired in Russian society for its street-smarts and survivor's instincts. And yet, ironically, while acknowledged as intelligent, many Russians interviewed are embarrassed by them: "Before perestroika, before our impoverished state after the collapse of the Soviet regime, we had no stray dogs. We had to push our dogs out of our homes because we couldn't feed ourselves, much less them and now they are breeding everywhere. They are a symbol for our impoverished and cruel state of affairs" (Igor, 2016). While tales of strays before perestroika exist, it is true that many citizens simply set their pets free and it was not uncommon to see pure bred dogs roaming in search of their homes in the 1990s. The situation got so bad that, it was said by students interviewed, dvorniashkis were simply shot in the streets by police to reduce the numbers. Under the Soviet regime certainly, populations of stray dogs were regulated:

There were teams that would destroy animals when members of the public asked for it . . . only the most quiet dogs survived . . . strays were sometimes turned into fur caps or used in scientific experiments . . . the most famous Soviet strays were Belka and Strelka, who are said to have lived near the space-medicine institute prior to being launched into orbit. (McGrane, 2013)

Acts of violence toward street dogs has been seen by some as a necessity, while others feel it is unnecessary and even damaging violence that begets violence and ultimately damages those who are privy to the acts.

The tensions surrounding street dogs today and tensions surrounding dog ownership in Russia has been described as a reflection of Russia's historical and political tensions and growing pains (Nelson in Pregowski, 2016). While under the Tsarist regime, those who could afford to do so kept companion animals, under the Bolsheviks pets were denounced as "decadent diversions of the exploiting classes" and the "parasitical lap-dogs" as well as homeless strays were marked as harmful to social progress (Nelson in Pregowski, 2016). Relations and attitudes of humans to their companion animals, their acceptance or rejection of all, some or none, is symbolic of struggles between the individual and society and in the social development of modernizing Russia.

Today, dvorniashki roam freely and their behaviors, such as their ability to navigate the metro system in Moscow, are seen as worthy of scholarly investigation. Their urban survival has been impressive, especially given the freezing temperatures in the winter. Vendors grow attached to the strays at markets and feed them while the metro offers warmth, shelter, and a means of transportation. As Neuronov, a researcher on the subject of Moscow's street dogs, reports:

> There are three models of metro dogs . . . dogs who live in the subway but do not travel, dogs who use the subway to travel short distances instead of walking, and entrepreneurial dogs who spend the day riding back and forth, busking. This last type of dog takes long trips, working the crowd for treats and emotional contact. (McGrane, 2013)

While humans need affection, apparently some dvorniashki crave human affection and, according to Neuronov, are especially attracted to women vendors over forty (McGrane, 2013).

The use of dogs as workers continues to be valued in Russian society. When strolling in larger parks, it is not uncommon to find a police dog agility course with opportunities for dogs to climb, jump, and balance. This equipment is offered to aid in the training for Schutzhund, a popular pastime for dog owners. Most of the people interviewed who had trained dogs, and even those who worked with their dogs, completed the initial training by sending their dogs to a school, if they could afford it. Practice came on a daily basis, as those living in Moscow and other urban areas could not allow their dogs, especially the larger breeds, to be unruly on the streets or in elevators. Breeders often sell their dogs with basic commands, but at a price not afforded by many.

The concept of well-being as an outcome of human-animal interaction is in nascent form in Russia. Historically, Russians have been proud of their working dogs as hunters of bears, guard dogs, and most recently explosive detection dogs. Breeds were and continue to be specifically developed for these jobs. While not bred specifically for therapy, attempts at using dogs to help children can be found as early as the 1940s. During this time of Soviet development an emphasis was placed on education and rehabilitation of homeless children and children with behavioral issues for which dogs were employed. This use of dogs became known as "canis terapia" in the 1990s. Therapy dogs were first used in Russian medical establishments after 2000.

When asked about the use of dogs as therapists, Russians interviewed felt it was a natural phenomenon as dogs "since tribal times have been the sputnik of humans and can (when well behaved) naturally calm those who are in their surroundings . . . also their body temperature is higher so of course they are a natural heater and conducive to helping relax the muscles of, say, a child with muscle spasms" (Taravikova, 2012). The use of pets for working specifically with mute children and those suffering from autistic spectrum disorder has also become a well-known therapy process in twenty-first-century Russia: "Dogs have a capacity to understand humans without words. They can decipher human body language, gestures and postures which helps establish contact with non-verbal patients such as those with autism" (Taravikova, 2012). No longer do people seem concerned about the potential negative powers dogs might possess due to their psychic proximity to natural forces and the spiritual world, rather, their closeness to nature and absence of evil that humans receive from society's negative impact, increases their ability to help us become better communicators, emotionally balanced, and better humans. In modern Russia the use of dogs for well-being represents a new development, an outcome of changing attitudes toward the meaning of the dog in Russian society as a whole. That being said, while animals as therapists are appreciated, much as in pre-soviet times, companion animals continue to mark status of individuals and represent the material aspirations of post-soviet society.

Animal Assisted Therapy is being used increasingly in other Eastern European countries as well. In Romania, for example, studies are being conducted to enhance recovery for patients by introducing dog-therapy and other animal facilitated treatment plans. Studies on including dog therapy teams (handler and animal) to improve focus, speech, neurological spasms, and behavioral issues are growing, and thus adding to the cross-cultural database of similar efforts. Of particular interest has been improving speech in children diagnosed with autistic spectrum disorder (ASD) (Grigore and Rusu, 2014). Whereas only a decade ago bringing animals into homes was regarded as odd in countries such as Romania, today initiatives to rescue animals from the streets, mitigate animal abuse, and accept them as sentient beings is growing (interview with Moore, 2016). Instead of disregarding cats and dogs, they are now seen as potential healers of medical issues that humans alone cannot alleviate.

CONCLUSION

It is undeniable that our animal healers are employed on a global basis in countries that have taken to keeping animals as companions. However, the specific cultural histories of welcoming animals as healers and contributors to human welfare are unique with nuanced beliefs in the capacities of animals. From medical findings of physiological responses to animals to beliefs in the spiritual powers of animals, societies present culturally unique approaches to integrating animals into their equally unique beliefs and practices surrounding healing and well-being. Examples in this chapter are taken from subcultures in the United States, Japan, and countries in selected countries in Europe, with a focus on Russia, to explore the developments of cultural attitudes toward pets in general, but also to demonstrate similarities that have evolved as the concept of animal as healer, employable for service, and as therapist, is spreading globally.

Even though the outcome of animals being held as pets or used for service may be similar across cultures, the ways in which societies come to their understandings of companion and service animals are individual. This chapter has investigated the importance of understanding culture, which includes history, language, religion, mythology, and literature, to fully comprehend developing trends in human-animal relations in specific social contexts. In the next chapter, we examine more fully one aspect of culture, that of language, to better understand the complexity of our relationships with animals and the meanings we give them in parts of Europe and the United States. As a result of the following discussion, we hope to entice future scholars to look more deeply into how other societies communicate with animals in order to better understand human-animal relationships cross-culturally and to further the well-being of both humans and animals.

NOTE

1. Cats also play a prominent role in Russian literature. Less has been written on the subject but I would recommend beginning with Mikhail Bulgakov's *Master and Margarita* (1966).

Chapter Three

Well-Being through Communication with and about Our Pets

Our ability to communicate is the foundation of establishing relationships, not only with other humans but also with animals. We naturally seek communication, driven by our predisposition to desire connectedness to those around us, a feeling we achieve when we believe we are communicating effectively, deeply and positively. In this chapter, we will investigate the role of communication and the effects of miscommunication with our companion animals, in particular dogs. After looking at examples of both communication and miscommunication gathered from interviews, we examine contradictory human behavior toward pets, as we, on the one hand, treat them as material possessions and, on the other, assign personhood to them. We discuss how such contradictory treatment of animals affect both human and animal emotional well-being. This chapter also explores the benefits of avoiding miscommunication by understanding our pets' true motivations. Finally, we engage the reader to consider the Rucksack Effect, a term coined by Nommensen, that is critical to understanding how dogs respond to us. Through stories from the author's veterinary practice in Germany, we decipher the complexity of animal behavior and communication and arrive at the ultimate insight, the interconnectedness of humans and their pets.

THE PET AS BOTH MATERIAL POSSESSION AND PERSON

We begin this chapter with a story that will help us to understand more clearly the underlying cultural motivations and effects of our contradictory behavior toward pets.

Melissa's story:

> Melissa, fresh out of college and having found a paid internship, wanted a dog—a small size creature that she could carry in a purse. "I think those little dogs, like Katy Perry's dog Butters, are cute. I could take it places and care for it like a baby." Melissa liked to shop and dress up herself and together, they would make a charming pair. She looked forward to the attention she and her pup would get. She envisioned her quality of life improving as her need to nurture a small, baby-like being would be fulfilled. Moreover, she would feel better as she would be able to obtain a certain work-life balance as she would need to be there for the dog in the evenings, preventing her from staying out too late. (Melissa, 2015)

Melissa's story is an example of the way in which people in modern day societies can treat animals as a result of cultural influences, including social media, fashion, and film. Depending on the historical time, place, and values of human societies, how humans have involved animals in their lives has changed due to social and cultural developments and cultural expressions of values. The ways in which humans interact with companion animals symbolize the values, beliefs, and customs in societies at specific times in history. In other words, society's traditions and ideals are reflected in the roles we assign to our pets and how we treat them. In many of today's complex societies, values glamorized by the media become internalized by individuals and nourish narratives about what it means to be happy and fulfilled. Material possessions are the obvious examples which many strive to obtain to gain a feeling of accomplishment, of having more than one's basic needs met. We see images of famous people who, to some, represent the heroes of our times, and whom many strive to emulate. Both Melissa's efforts to imitate her heroes and her personal desire to nurture is motivated by social expectations represented in various forms of media. As pointed out in the field of psychology, the need to nurture is not simply a matter of some women being hardwired to do so, but women being socialized from girlhood throughout their life (Walker, 2011). As a result, narratives, as the one told by Melissa, are repeated daily by young women in societies around the world.

Melissa's story demonstrates a contradictory relationship we hold with our pets which involves a tradition of, on the one hand, objectifying pets and on the other, assigning personhood to animals. Personhood is defined varyingly in the social sciences as a concept unique to individual cultures. It is a state that, in its most basic definition, refers to a sentient and social state of being, one that changes, depending on context and power relations. To achieve personhood is to achieve the status of a full-fledged member of society. Depending on cultural expectations, personhood develops in stages and frequently symbolically realized through rituals and rites of passage such as those in which youth attains adulthood. Animals can also go through rites of passage in human society, obtaining status as more or less socialized and even titled to work among humans. A "Companion Dog" can officially receive a title as such if and when she passes the various tests for the American Kennel Association. A service animal receives a job after a distinct education and testing, with a ceremony marking the moment. That being said, while animals may achieve a degree of personhood conferred upon them by humans, humans also treat their animals as they might a material possession.

Objectification of animals is reinforced in the way we relate to our animals by "utilizing" them, and in the language we use to talk about them. For example, by using the word "pet" we signify our companion animals are owned possessions. A pet is: "an animal kept for pleasure . . . property of their human owner" (Hurn, 2012, p. 98). While pet owners might acknowledge the value of companionship and even family membership, as Hurn points out, "the socio-cultural (and legally sanctioned) expectation is that pets belong to individual humans who have certain responsibilities toward these animals, but also the power over the animal's life and death" (p. 98). The concept of pet affects how we behave toward certain animals and encourages beliefs that the human-pet relationship is based on human domination over a pet, a form of speciesism.

While a prominent perspective in North America and Europe, the way in which we think about pets is by no means global, just as the definition of what makes an animal a companion animal differs from one country to the next. As one study concludes: "There seems to be no deeper answer to the question of what different peoples focus on—specific, and surprising, features—to qualify creatures as 'exotic' or 'friendly,' 'dangerous' or 'illegal' other than pervasive cultural commitments" (Waller in Pregowski, 2017, p. 24). Cultural factors, including religion and traditions, expressed in literature and other forms of media, shape our attitudes and behaviors toward our companion animals differently throughout the world.

The owner-pet model of human-animal relations found in many complexes of the twenty-first century is one that perpetuates the victimization of animals. Historically, the concept of a pet pays little heed to the true effects on the animal and reflects a Western worldview of approaching others and, in this case, non-human animals in an us-them manner, denying them characteristics that would make them the "same" including the ability to reason, to have dignity, the ability to love and, by extension, similar rights such as human rights. At the very least, humans see nature as something to be used. It is as if all natural things and beings were created to serve human needs. Early twentieth-century German philosopher, Martin Heidegger, analyzed the phenomenon of humans treating all of nature as if it were on call for us to use (Heidegger, 2001, p. 8).

There is no one definition of personhood across cultures and it remains a concept that is widely debated both theoretically and in practice. Some scholars do not acknowledge personhood of animals: "personhood as a state of being is not open to nonhuman animal kinds" (Ingoldt in Hurn, 2012, p. 30). Such a perspective pervades much of the social sciences when "person" is equated with "human." By not ascribing personhood to non-humans, objectification of non-human animals is condoned: "if we are raised within a cultural context where 'person' equals 'human' we will expect, or rather be expected, to see humans and only humans as persons, regardless of whether or not our experience of non-human others leads us to doubt this premise" (p. 30). In other words, we are culturally locked into denying personhood to non-humans, which has rather profound implications for the well-being of the pet.

Yet, if we venture to define personhood as simply an animate, self-conscious being that develops in social contexts through interactions with others, then personhood of animals is revealed through interactions with humans. Indeed, for many people this is precisely the case, as we assign the status of family membership, friendship, even partnership to our pets. However, our relationship is problematized as we also continue to objectify them, to own them and in many a sad case, victimize them. Ironically, while on the one hand many find it hard to assign personhood to non-human animals, on the other, we build relationships with them and assume they possess a human-like psychology.

At some point in history, domestication as cohabitation was not enough for us. We realized that we could get more out of our animals and that one thing in particular was needed for this to happen: a relationship. Human craving for relationships is fostered by an innate tendency to empathize and value empathy from other live beings. We seek connections with others and thrive on mutual understanding. It is a mechanism for survival and an ingredient of contentment and happiness. As one animal behaviorist explains: "Understanding what someone else is experiencing is the key to feeling connected, and feeling connected is an integral part of any good relationship. 'Penny for your thought' is more than an old-fashioned phrase—it's an expression of our desire to understand the thoughts and emotions of those we love. We humans are social animals, and our desire for connection is deep and relentless" (McConnel, 2007, xxiii). As social animals, we survive by connecting with others, seeking empathy and explanations for behavior of others' actions. Similarly, we crave this connection with our pets and work to establish a meaningful relationship with them.

Unfortunately, our desire to connect with our pets has led us down a slippery slope of anthropomorphizing. As we gaze into the eyes of our pets, we study them, try to understand them and to empathize. Empathy is based on an ability to see things from another's point of view and for this we have relied heavily on our instinct, which may not always be correct. Without the average person's ability to conduct scientific research and enter the brain of the dog on a given day, we are quick to project ourselves reflected in the pet. We thus engage in a relationship in which we assume the animal understands us, reads our emotions and thoughts, and in turn we believe to understand the motivation behind their behavior. In other words, people assume human responses to our human world as when we say a pet "knows she should xxx (fill in the blank with desirable behavior) but she is just being stubborn or paying me back for something I did" (McConnell, p. xxiii).

Indeed, who can fault us for assuming human-like perspectives of our pets? They have us fooled with seemingly appropriate human reactions:

> Robert loved his lab Freni and took her everywhere. His job as a contractor allowed him to do so. Sometimes, filled with enthusiasm for his pup, Robert would open his arms as he would approach bending over her to smother her with love and affection. She would respond with her ears back, looking oh so cute, licking her lips as if ready to give kisses to Robert, her tail wagging faster every second, tightly close to her legs, ultimately flipping on her back "to receive belly rubs," Robert explained. His only lament: "how she piddles when she is happy to see me." (Pay, 2015)

There is no denying that Robert and Freni have a close bond. However, his interpretation of her reaction is more of a description of how he could identify with her feelings (having them himself) than how an animal behaviorist would analyze her response. The ears back? A sign of submission. The tail wagging fast as if tightly wound especially in combination with urination? According to behaviorist Turid Rugaas, a scholar of canine body language, it is a "white flag," signaling peace, trying to make you calm down (Rugaas, 2006, p. 36). In other words, Freni is stressed. And how about licking as if giving air kisses? This is a very common behavior for dogs as well in reaction to anticipation of people bending over them or holding them tightly. It is another calming signal (p. 14), and again, a sign of stress.

In the context of understanding animal behavior, it behooves us to dig more deeply into this theme. In order for a person to relate to an animal, it is practically impossible not to anthropomorphize. We need to feel we understand and empathize in order to trust. Anthropomorphizing is a natural human inclination as it offers a seemingly logical way to analyze animals. However, our ability to step back and critically examine animal behavior is essential to ensuring a realistic and healthy relationship with our pets as opposed to a relationship in which human or animal or both suffer.

During our research in one practice in Germany, we began our discussions by asking clients what role the pet plays in a client's life? The most frequent answers collected included:

- My pet is my soulmate
- My pet is my life—I prefer him to any human being

- My pet is my partner, he protects me
- My pet is my baby/child

As we discovered, pets fulfill many roles, roles that are foreign to their species (such as taking on the role of a human baby) and of which they have limited comprehension. Interesting to the authors, is that the animal behaviorists and veterinarians learn not only what the pet is supposed to be to a particular human, but also what a particular person might be missing in life. The result is that the role of the behaviorist evolves into working with the human client equally intensively, sometimes in tandem with a psychological therapist, as with the animal in question. Such was the case with a client, Ms. B., who reached out to Nommensen because her seven-year-old West Highland Terrier, Nino, barked too much, to the point that the neighbors complained. Ms. B. was terribly worried about losing her apartment. Nommensen recalls:

> We met at her house so that I could understand the context and environment in which the unwanted behavior was taking place. Upon entering her home I immediately noticed a mattress with sheets, the owner's bed, I found out, in the entrance hall. To make a rather long story short, it turned out that the barking of the dog was only a small problem among a larger one: Nino had taken the role of boss by taking over the bedroom, controlling the entrance to the kitchen and terrace and claiming the sofa in the living room. For approximately six years, Ms. B. slept in the hall, sat on the floor to watch television and was constantly being nipped in her legs when she tried to enter the kitchen. After convincing Ms. B. that her relationship with Nino was unhealthy, she agreed to make changes. It took two years of behavior modification before Nino allowed his owner to move back into the bedroom, use the couch and cook at ease in her kitchen. With new rules in place, even the constant barking ceased. Ms. B., in allowing her dog to take over in the relationship, had lost a healthy perspective on animal-human relations to the point that she had forgotten what it meant to live comfortably. (Nommensen, 2015)

By anthropomorphizing, humans confuse both their animals and themselves, detracting from the mutual benefits that are possible.

Author and animal behaviorist, Donaldson (1996) has given a list of the many misguided assumptions we make in the context of training a dog (for a complete list and discussion see Donaldson, 1996, pp. 34–36). We tend to assume that what should be seen as an under-motivated or undertrained dog's behavior is due to any number of things other than not being trained or motivated. The list includes:

1. The dog is being dominant
2. The dog is being spiteful
3. The dog is being stubborn

4. The dog is too excited
5. The dog is in a bad mood or tired
6. The dog is over-trained (which is the author's favorite)
7. The behavior is breed related

While dogs have feelings of dominance and can be excitable and easily distracted, a well-trained and motivated dog will not let those emotions get the better of her. Many of the emotions we assign to our dogs are simply assumptions that our dogs react as we do or we take the concept of being alpha to an extreme. Being a good leader, teacher, and team member for your dog requires an educated reading of canine signals.

All this is not to say that dogs are complete aliens. Indeed, as stated, they have many emotions like us. Wohlleben has described this likeness most extensively in his book *Das Seelenleben der Tiere* (The Soul-Life of Animals) (2016) in which he writes: "The more I looked, the more I discovered in the supposed uniquely human emotions in pets and their wild kin in the forest . . . Wherever one turns, animals love, empathize and live with passion" (translated from Wohlleben, 2016, p. 8). His findings dare us to disagree.

The emotions we feel from petting a dog are similar to the feelings dogs experience when being petted. In the end, dogs and humans have learned one thing: we are good for each other when we understand each other. We know that dog + human = better life for human (when managed well) and not-so-bad life for dog and in some cases, quite exceptional for both.

A fine line exists between assigning status to a pet and to thinking of an animal as a contributing member to society. Once social status is achieved, humans easily fall into anthropomorphizing animals to the point that they misread and misjudge an animal's perceptions and reactions. Careful interspecies communication between humans and their companion animals is essential for a relationship to flourish.

In a sense, we need to understand not only the differences in species but also in cultures, that is the perceptions and behaviors that are shaped by the cultural contexts in which we are born. Donaldson (1996) discusses the culture clash between humans and dogs. She points out that the ways in which we do things such as solve confrontations in human culture is quite different than how a dog would:

> Aggressive behavior does not fracture relationships in dog society. It's all taken very much in stride. The problem is that aggression often changes things a great deal in dog-human relationships. We routinely execute dogs who bite. That's quite the culture clash. . . . Dogs are unaware that they have been adopted into a culture where biting is considered a betrayal of trust and a capital offense. (Donaldson, 1996, pp. 57–58)

If biting occurs, we as humans have failed to communicate our expectations. While this is an extreme case of miscommunication, it happens too many times each day and should force each and every one of us to reconsider anthropomorphizing.

Our dogs are admirable in that unlike most other species they have learned many of our behavior schemes, although their perceptions and inter-pretations of our schemes are not necessarily the same as ours. Dogs have developed social competence in our human world by being able to fit into society, mastering necessary skills including forming attachments, regulating aggression, learning many of our rules at home and on the streets, providing assistance and participating in group activities (Miklosi, 2015, p. 17). That being said, they have not mastered human language to the extent that they can communicate verbally with symbols or grammar the way we do. While they are able to communicate in complex and subtle ways, it is not the same as human communication. If we wish to make the relationship work, we need to sharpen our understanding of them and learn to communicate effectively with them.

HUMAN LANGUAGE MEETS CANINE LANGUAGE

In social scientific scholarship, there is much debate as to the whether or not human and animal forms of communication are completely distinct entities. Reflections on animal communication by Temple Grandin (2005) describes it in a way the authors of this book embrace: our communications systems are similar enough to put them on the same spectrum. In her words: "The differ-ence is quantitative, not qualitative. . . . It's time to start thinking about animals as capable and communicative beings. It's also time to stop making assumptions" (Grandin and Johnson, 2005, pp. 281–283). There is much to be learned from animals, not only about themselves, but about ourselves as well.

Human communication offers information (linguistically labeled the in-formative use of language) that can be true or false about events, or about objects or places the receiver may never have experienced, but is capable of imagining by decoding the symbolism of language. We can initiate or contin-ue a conversation of complex meanings through questions. We can evoke responses to varying degrees with commands or suggestions (the evocative use of language). We can evaluate based on moral and ethical judgments. We can even accomplish an act and perform it by simply saying it. We can, for example, apologize by saying "I apologize." While animals can certainly communicate similar information, their communication is, on a spectrum, less symbolically complex. Human symbolic communication offers unlimit-ed combinations of new ideas and communicative functions.

Unique to human language is indeed the symbolic complexity. In speech, for example, sounds stand for words that stand for actions and objects which can express numerous things at once (as in a statement that claims a fact and an emotion at the same time) and can take on aesthetic qualities as in poetry. Speakers can create intentional and unintentional reactions and emotions in the audience. Well-known linguist Searle sums it up:

> In a typical speech situation involving a speaker, a hearer, and an utterance by the speaker, there are many kinds of acts associated with the speaker's utterance. The speaker will characteristically have moved his jaw and tongue and made noises. In addition, he will characteristically have performed some acts within the class which includes informing or irritating or boring his hearers; he will further characteristically have performed acts within the class which includes referring to Kennedy or Kruschchev or the North Pole; and he will also have performed acts within the class which includes making statements, asking questions, issuing commands, giving reports, greetings and warnings. The members of this last class is . . . called illocutionary acts. (Searle, 1965, p. 221)

Our speech acts, the functions our utterances serve, depend on a wide variety of complex systems involving grammar, intonation, stress, mood, body language, context of the situation, and more.

Language not only serves to communicate ideas, it affects how we think about and how we experience the world. A basic example would be the naming of things. Gendering all nouns in some languages seems to affect how native speakers of such a language think about the object (Boroditsky et al., 2003). While a bridge is masculine in French (le pont), it is feminine in German (die Bruecke). When asked to describe le pont, French speakers tend to describe it as strong and masculine, whereas Germans spoke of die Bruecke by describing its beauty, elegance, and other feminine qualities. This idea that language affects how we perceive is based on Edward Sapir and Lee Whorf's findings in 1940 and has been called the Sapir-Whorf hypothesis. Their hypothesis points to a dimension of language that differentiates us from our dogs.

While it can be argued that animals also communicate symbolically, their communication is presented as a unitary whole, which cannot be creatively broken apart to convey separate units. As explained by linguist Stephen Anderson (2004) in his study of songbirds, vocalizations are complex, the signal has a unitary and holistic relation to the message it coveys, such as attracting a mate or signaling danger.

Whereas humans relate to each other through a combination of kinesics, speech and writing to exchange information, dogs rely mostly on body language. Vocalizations are used as supplements to nonverbal communication. It should be noted, however, that certain canine breeds such as German Shepherds and Dachshunds, utilize vocalizations (barking, howling, whimpering) more than others. The extent to which giving off scent as through sweat glands plays a role is not yet clear as such data is difficult to gather. In fact, the significance and extent of communication through scent has not been sufficiently researched and the authors believe that scent communication might be more important than all other forms. Horowitz (2016) recounts her research at the Dog Cognition Lab at Barnard College in New York in which she studied "the pet-dog's experience of himself, other dogs, and the smells of the human world in which he lives" (Horowitz, 2016, p. 3). Via her study the variety of canine olfactory abilities Horowitz opens a world of scent to the reader, much of which, as she writes, "is beyond our ability to sense, and some of which we simply need a guide to see" (Horowitz, 2016, p. 5). Even after this exploration, we find that there is more to learn when it comes to a dog's ability to perceive via scent.

Because of their focus on scent, dogs are used for a variety of jobs, including learning to react to changes in a human's sweat. The changes they are trained to detect are those that surpass what is considered healthy or "normal" for a particular person. This work is lifesaving, especially for people suffering from epilepsy or type one diabetes as well as other ailments. The training for such work is complex and takes time, not to mention the cost, but ultimately worthwhile for the dog's human.

Dogs have been trained to detect alterations in scent that could signal a patient's suicide. Joe is one example of a dog who worked in a psychiatric clinic and was trained to drop his leash, which he otherwise carried in his mouth, when he sensed a person's anxiety was reaching a critical point, indicating a person's emotional state that might lead to suicide. At this point the handler knew to engage in conversation with that person and to ascertain a way forward (Krauss, interview, Feb. 9, 2016).

Dogs combine all their senses to understand situations and among themselves, they are artists of communication—masters of their canine language and interpretation. They swiftly process complex signals and respond to each other, a necessity for safe coexistence in a pack. Initial contacts are often ritualized to avoid sudden fallouts. A dog uses his own version of a dialogue involving questions and answers through body language and scent with the other dog to discover the other's mood and basic emotional state.

Ritualized behavior becomes more complex as a dog works to express more complex intentions such as invitation to play. Dogs do in fact invite others to play by asking specific questions including: Can I come closer to learn more about you and how do you feel right now? Can we take the next step? One can only imagine how difficult it is in a group, especially if this group is already at play and new partners enter as in a dog park. Moreover, their preoccupation with reading each other extends to deciphering us humans: our canine companions are continuously scanning us and figuring us out.

As humans, we would most likely be overwhelmed by utilizing a variety of signals involving all the senses, but the dog accomplishes this seamlessly. Animal communicative rituals that allow the sending, receiving, and judging of collected information is socialized from birth and learned by each species. For this reason, experienced trainers require their dogs to experience diverse breeds at all ages, as each breed has its own nuanced pattern of communication. Early socialization leads to a more balanced and adaptable canine companion.

Miscommunication can occur when we wrongly accuse a perfectly sound canine interaction as problematic. The result can be confusing to dogs and lead to future communication difficulties among the dogs themselves, not to mention the trust between human and animal. A case in point is a common dog park encounter: two dogs engage playfully with one another. One is young and, after a while is corrected by the senior dog. The younger dog does not back away (as he should) and the corrections of the older dog become harsher. A third comes into the mix and begins to bark. The owner tells the dog to be quiet as the human wrongly interprets the loud behavior as aggression. In fact, the barking dog is announcing that mismanagement of the younger and older dog is taking place: continuous subduing of the younger one has limits and the owners of the other two should have protected the younger dog, rather than silencing the announcer. Humans tend to silence the loudest, often embarrassed by their dog's boisterous behavior, without recognizing the real intent of the dogs.

The result is that the young dog has become a victim who, in the future, may turn on the senior dog or become fearful. The older dog has learned to enjoy the role of regulator and has found encouragement through lack of intervention and may strike this behavior up a notch in the future. The announcer has learned that barking is insufficient and may require harsher engagement the next time.

The learning process continues throughout the lives of dogs, as they continue to determine each other's nuanced iterations or even dialects in canine language as well as human intervention. Continuous exposure to other dogs and people is thus important since, as with humans, language training ensures competence and fluency.

Human-dog interaction and communication must be practiced throughout the life of the dog. Even in an active play situation between dogs, our dogs send signals to us with questions and answers. Watch as they look up, come back to you to check in, ensure you are still where you were. It is worth emphasizing that it is precisely the success of reading our companion's body language that enriches our mutual relationship and feelings of trust and connectedness we need to achieve well-being. The authors of this book work daily to strengthen communication, read signals, learn our companions' inclinations and habits, to read their body language and their potential reactions to specific situations, both in human and canine contexts. We also ensure daily exposure of our dogs with human society and have the fortune of having dogs who can go on search and rescue missions as well as offer therapy to ailing individuals.

Knowing how a dog might react or respond strengthens not only our mutual understanding, but also a sense of balance and emotional health. Dogs live in the moment, completely mindful—a state that many of us strive to achieve with great effort through such activities as yoga and meditation. Learning to live in the moment through our canine companions can help our memory and analysis of the past, understanding of the present, and potential of the future. Mindfulness goes beyond the visible signs, along with the smells and sensations we experience.

Mindfulness is present in our canine companions as they assess us moment to moment. Not only our body language, but also our scent changes signal our emotional state: neutral, fear, discomfort, joy, to name a few.

> Ben and his dog, Max, a Labrador retriever puppy, had an unpleasant encounter at the dog park: Max was playing with his ball when another dog, ran and grabbed it. Max and the other dog had a tussle, but luckily no-one was injured. The next day, as they enter the park, Ben is worried. He looks for the other dog. Max makes contact with the first dog with no problem but in that moment, Ben reacts by coming closer to protect Max and to control the situation. It is at this point that Max tenses up. (observations by Nommensen, 2015)

When encountering other dogs in any context, your feelings about the situation are clear to the dog. If you do not feel in control and you have a dog that tends to take your signals as more reliable than his own intuition, his attitude toward the new pack will be negative. It is as if Ben was carrying his concern in a heavy rucksack, which Max could easily sense. We all carry a rucksack of experiences, good and bad, to which we refer for quick solutions. In this case, Max was relaxed until Ben came closer and displayed his tension. Because Max no longer trusts his own judgment of the situation and takes his leader's intuition as more accurate, positive interaction between the dogs is halted. Had Ben zipped his rucksack, so to speak, Max would certainly have been more relaxed.

Nommensen's concept of the "emotional rucksack" is one that warrants further analysis, which we offer in chapter 5. For now we present here a few stories to clarify what we mean and how we can rid ourselves from such a burden either with the aid of psychological insight or with the help of our four-legged companions.

THE EMOTIONAL RUCKSACK EFFECT

Our rucksack is important for survival, as it helps us assess new situations based on previous experiences, allowing us to make necessary judgment calls. But we do have the choice to close the rucksack, when need be. Here are some stories that might bring this rucksack concept closer to you.

> A few years ago, a dog owner asked me to help her with her beautiful female Papillion: Her dog refused her meals. The lady had tried everything, changing the food and cooking for the dog and even hand-feeding her precious pup, all to no avail. The situation became critical as the dog began to suffer from malnutrition and was set up with calorie infusions. My immediate impression was that the dog was indeed hungry, but that the owner was the one who was suffering, exasperated, as she pushed food, beginning at 6AM and from there-on regularly every half hour until the evening.
>
> Upon further questioning, I learned that her previous dog, who had passed quite a number of years prior to this situation, had suffered from pancreatitis and needed to be spoon-fed throughout the day. The owner could not maintain the rigorous schedule 24-7 and had to have her beloved dog put down. Her new love, the Papillion, at first had no issues eating until around the age of three months. (Nommensen 2016)

What could have been the cause of this sudden refusal to eat? As it turned out, the owner had merged her fears about her previous dog with her relationship to the new puppy and continued the feeding ritual. The puppy was overwhelmed by the pressure of this regime and her natural feeding rhythm was completely disrupted leading to her outright refusal of food. As soon as the owner acknowledged this harmful pattern for both human and animal, she was able to "zip her rucksack" so-to-speak and began a new routine of putting out food and ignoring the dog's feeding. With this method, the Papillion reawakened her internal feeding rhythm and, as I write this story, has no food issues. By acknowledging our most distant experiences, we can understand and change our relationship with our dog.

Another story that helps to demonstrate the ability of dogs to help relieve us of our inhibitions is about Lea and her family.

> Lea was, at the time I knew her, ten years old and suffered since birth from Asperger Syndrome. Despite her challenges, Lea was a child full of spirit and the energizer in her family. She was open to those dear to her, but more closed off to strangers. Even though the family had offered Lea all the support they could, her ability to engage socially was not improving. Her parents dreamed of sending Lea to an integrated school, but her inability to navigate through large numbers of people and independently kept her at home.
>
> And so the idea was born that Lea needed a dog. Her family had always wanted a pet and the idea of a dog was welcomed. No more than a month later, a beautiful female retriever, Kira, moved in and Lea was taught to care for

Kira and attend dog school. The two became a good team and Lea began to blossom. One day, on a walk with the family, Lea was approached by a couple: They thought Lea and Kira were adorable together and asked what the dog's name was. To the parents' surprise, Lea answered without hesitation and even added Kira's age and breed.

Lea continued to feel at ease with strangers with Kira at her side. Moreover, her speech improved and her ability to feel secure and at ease in public grew. Her parents had Kira trained as a therapy dog so that the team could enter the integrated school. The initial step towards Lea's future to grow among her peers was made. (Nommensen)

Lea's story demonstrates that the attachment to an animal can bring to light potentials in humans that had previously been dismissed as impossible. Kira, simply through her presence, enabled Lea to gain a sense of worth and security.

Our final story demonstrates the nurturing bond we hold with our pets, how our emotional burden can be reflected in their behavior and how we can work to appreciate and also manage their deep insight into our psyche.

Anette had been visiting our practice for years with her female dog Leila. Our relationship was based on yearly check-ups and so I had not gotten to know her all that well. After a few years, Anette's life changed dramatically: her husband died in a car accident. We learned about this at her visit, right after the tragedy and so we took some time to listen. Anette went into great detail about the accident and was extremely happy that she still had Leila: "She is for me my rock. Without her, I might have given up on life."

A few days later I saw her again, only this time at my dog-training school. She wanted to register for a new course and she noted that her dog's behavior had changed significantly in the last days. Prior to the accident, Leila was a happy, stable dog who could play on her own for some time. After the accident, Leila stayed close to Anette. While she continued to play, it was always within Anette's sight and followed Anette throughout the house. Anette noticed that whenever she felt sad, Leila would stand close by her side and touch her. (Nommensen)

How can this behavior change be explained? Leila was able to discern Anette's change in demeanor and answered this with proximity and control. Leila no longer trusted Anette to manage in different contexts. Leila's response was to build body contact whenever Anette became more emotional and became a barometer that measured the intensity of Anette's mourning at any given time.

On the one hand, Anette enjoyed this closeness, but on the other hand, it bothered her that she could not leave without a reaction from her dog. At last, through training, we were able to normalize and balance her relationship with her dog.

This last story depicts our close ties to our animals and how, like in a pack, dogs work hard to establish emotional balance between pack members. Stark changes in pack behavior based on emotional imbalances can lead to unpredictable reactions, which in turn can threaten the well-being of the pack. Leila was deeply engaged in bringing stability back through physical closeness, a method dogs use to control situations. The ability for dogs to read us, understand our emotions and to nurture us as best they can, never ceases to amaze even the most experienced behaviorist and scholar of human and animal cultures. It is the springboard we now take to delve more deeply into healing abilities and benefits to both humans and animals in the following chapters.

The ability to read our animals and to make ourselves clear to them has benefits beyond the relationship built between the owner and pet and the sense of contentment this relationship brings. Understanding animals can have lasting effects in the development of children and ultimately on society. Research has pointed to the fact that carefully exposing children at a young age to animals is beneficial. Asking children to relate to animals, care for animals, and live with animals increases their level of social competence and empathy. Many other results include:

- Children who had a pet during their childhood were more empathetic, more prone to enter a helping profession, and were more oriented toward social values than those without a pet.
- Children who had increased empathy scores because of their relationship with their pets also showed greater empathy toward people.
- Ten-year-old children who had established strong bonds with their dog had significantly higher self-esteem, as well as greater empathy.
- When a dog was present in the classroom of first graders, they showed higher social integration and less aggression compared to children in a classroom without an animal.

These individualized benefits during childhood necessarily lead to less violence as they grow up and integrate into society. On the flip side, children who have been known to mistreat animals have shown to develop aggressive behavioral tendencies (Doris Day Animal Foundation, accessed February 2017).

Effective and compassionate human-animal communication, when achieved, is the foundation for our ability to give, develop, and receive a multitude of benefits leading to our sense of happiness, contentment, and a deeper understanding of ourselves and others.

Chapter Four

Mutual Benefits through Human-Animal Contact and Training: What Science and Personal Narratives Tell

There is no doubt that our lives with our companion animals are enriched in complex ways. Pets bring us joy and help us through difficult moments, they keep us physically fit and help us to engage socially. Many people interviewed for this project describe their pets as friends and family members. Such designations should not be underestimated as they point to the depth of human relationships with animals. In instances where a bond between human and animal functions well, life is good. However, such close bonding risks not satisfying both animal and human needs 100 percent of the time. In this chapter, we will examine the joys and mutual enrichments of these relationships while bearing in mind the problems that can arise. We begin with a discussion of what it means to be bonded with an animal, in particular with dogs, and move to a discussion of the benefits animals receive from our relationship with them.

BENEFITS HUMANS RECEIVE FROM THE HUMAN-ANIMAL BOND

Many dog owners with whom we are professionally engaged have expressed that, without their four-legged companions, they might not venture outdoors. Dogs and other companion animals, including horses, compel us to engage with the outdoors, not only helping us maintain a healthy cardiovascular system, but also bringing us in touch with nature as we increase our awareness of seasonal transformations—the blossoming in the fields, the foliage on the ground, and corresponding smells and sensations, and so forth.

Beyond awakening the senses, illnesses such as diabetes, rheumatoid arthritis, and migraines have been mitigated with the help of dogs. German cardiologist, Kopernick (2013) notes the value of dogs and other animals, such as horses, that compel humans to go out to properly care for them. Through consistent outdoor exercise, no matter the weather, we are able to strengthen our immune system and combat eventual health hazards. The lead-doctor at the clinic for cardiologic rehabilitation in Duisburg, Germany, Ralf Jordan, indicates a mere 150 minutes of movement outdoors per week can improve the cardio-vascular system. Dogs allow us to meet this threshold easily and enjoyably (Kopernick, 2013).

A number of those interviewed commented that they would never venture out without a dog at my side. So one: "My dog gives me a reason beyond myself to take a walk outdoors. Perhaps this is due to our German upbringing. We commonly say that without a reason, why should we venture out?"

Walking a dog also leads to another positive result: a faster and easier way to come into contact with other people, people we may have never noticed or engaged with otherwise. Here a dog bridges the social hurdles of introductions and building of relationships. Of course, this works better without a greeting of muddy paws on the newcomer. An untrained or unsocialized dog who displays aggressive behavior can just as easily elicit a negative reaction. As you might discern, we, the authors, speak from personal experience.

A number of studies point to the positive effects of companion animals on human well-being. We will abstain from a tedious enumeration of them all, but instead focus on a few that stand out. One name in particular, Erika Friedmann, appears most frequently in our research on the subject. As an American sociologist she, along with Thomas (1980) researched the effects of human relationships on heart attack patients. In this study, patients were asked to fill out a questionnaire about their life-style, family, children, the quality of their marriage or partnership, hobbies, and the like. Questions were asked about pets, initially only to cover all possible variables. As a result, Friedmann found no correlation between human relationships and healing and recovery from illnesses. Rather, her questions and resulting answers did indicate rather surprising correlations. After twelve months following the same patients beyond their hospital stays, Friedmann found that those who had pets were able to reenter their normal daily lives more quickly than those without pets, regardless of what species of pet they owned. One possible explanation could be that pet owners feel responsible for the well-being of their pets and are therefore motivated to return to their everyday routine, which in turn requires them to heal quickly after an illness. The strength of human will cannot be underestimated. As an example, one interviewee demonstrated a similar phenomenon: Heide, a woman in her fifties, was quick to return to her regular walks after hip replacement surgery. Her physical therapists were amazed and credited her dog Josie as the motivation for her fast rehabilitation. In fact, the physician had never witnessed such a rapid recovery in patients with similar operations.

Heide herself explains: "I don't enjoy being dependent on strange people and certainly not for taking care of Josie, so the sooner I got back to walking my dog, the better" (A. Heidemarie, interview, January 16, 2017).

Perhaps most interesting in Friedmann's findings was the fact that not all animals have the same effect on patients' recovery. Dog owners had a quicker recovery from their surgeries than, for example, cat owners. They further discovered that the average life expectancy after one year was 8.6 times greater for dog owners than for patients without a pet. These findings proved to be both astounding and hard to explain. Katcher, Lynch, Beck, and Friedmann (1983) found a correlation a few years later: People who, on a daily basis with either their own or another's pet engaged in bodily contact through petting and touching, developed lower blood pressure and pulse than people without such contact (Katcher, 1983; Katcher et al., 1983; Vormbrock and Gossberg, 1988). Similarly, the cortisol level, a hormone triggered in the body during stressful periods, was lowered. Thus, it has been scientifically confirmed that contact with animals has a calming effect. Moreover, such contact evokes feelings of trust and security (de Smet, 1992; Greiffenhagen, 1991; Katcher, 1983). The reason for this is the hormone oxytocin, which is triggered through bodily contact, evoking feelings of bonding between partners.

Oxytocin is an incredibly powerful hormone which is also known as the "bonding" hormone. It forms in an important part of our brain, the hypothalamus, which is responsible for the processing of events that evoke emotional responses. Certain social interactions trigger the production of oxytocin resulting in a sense of bonding. We can witness its power during breastfeeding, when oxytocin is expressed at a higher rate in both mother and child. Aiding in this process is also the role of touch, which explains the correlation between petting and heightened well-being among humans and animals. One can go so far as to say it is at this point, with the surge in oxytocin, that imprinting occurs. Without petting, the relationship between human and animal is less intense. For example, people who have aquariums do not express oxytocin while watching their fish. That being said, pet fish do elevate a sense of well-being (Katcher, 1983).

One of many significant studies on the power of oxytocin was conducted in Japan by the scientist Takefumi Kikusui, an animal behaviorist who set out to study to what extent oxytocin leads to maternal bonding, trust and altruism:

Kikusui convinced 30 dog owners to bring their pets into his lab. The researchers persuaded two "wolf" owners to participate in the study as well. The first step was to collect urine from both human and dogs that participated. After that, the owners, couples, were asked to interact and pet their dogs for about 30 minutes. When time was up, the team took urine samples again. Both male and female owners had a 300% rise in oxytocin levels. The only exceptions were the two owners who had brought their wolves. They did no experience any change in oxytocin levels, which was explained by the fact that during petting, they had not had eye contact with the wolves. In the second experiment, they repeated the same procedure, except this time they gave the dogs a nasal spray of oxytocin before they were allowed to interact with their owners. Female dogs that were given the nasal spray showed up to 150% more eye contact to their owners whereas the spray had no impact on the male dogs or the wolves. Kikusui concluded that human/dog interactions elicit the same type of oxytocin feedback loop as seen between mothers and their infants. "This positive feedback loop . . . may have played a critical role in dog domestication . . . only those that could bond with humans would have received care and protection" (David Grimm 2015). It was also noted that oxytocin made dogs friendlier toward other dogs. Beyond reproduction, oxytocin was found to improve and maintain close social relationships both within and between species. (Morell, 2014)

Through interacting with dogs, both humans and animals are rewarded. With eye contact, the reward is even greater. The result is that humans feel the need to nurture our pets and dogs are motivated to seek both eye and body contact with humans.

Because of such scientifically established positive effects on humans, animals have been indispensable in therapy for patients with phobias, a topic to be discussed later in the book. What is essential for effective treatment of patients is the bodily contact with animals, preferably with furry ones. While an aquarium with fish can also have a calming effect, it is not as strong as animals which can be touched.

REDUCED STRESS AND PET OWNERSHIP

Oxytocin is also responsible for the reduction of stress and fear, leading to a feeling of trust and safety (Unvas-Moberg et al., 1999; Uvnas-Moberg and Petersson, 2005; Uvnas-Moberg et al., 2005; Uvnas-Moberg et al., 2011). Pet owners in general have an easier time in regulating the triggering of cortisol, the hormone that is produced in response to stress (Allen et al., 2002). They react more slowly to stressful situations, which leads to a slower accumulation of stress hormones in the blood as interactions with pets increases Cortisol levels.

Moreover, it appears that pet owners have the possibility of training their hormonal production on a daily basis as they engage with their animals and learn to calm themselves (Friedmann et al., 1983). It is for this reason that animal therapy has become an effective treatment for reduction in stress and anxiety.

As mentioned in chapter I, beyond the therapeutic benefits such as helping people recuperate from physical ailments, animals, especially dogs, can act as catalysts for people who have difficulty socializing and exploring their surroundings. Many find that their pet at their side enables them to go places they dare not tread alone. People who suffer from phobias, depression, or other destabilizing psychological differences feel more accepted and valued with an animal at their side. As one psychologist explains:

> In relationships, for example, with family members and loved ones that are complicated—a pet can be a great antidote. With a pet you can just feel—you don't have to worry about the pets feelings getting hurt or getting advice you don't want—and taking care of a pet gives you a sense of your own value and importance. Also having a daily schedule helps people with depression for example—there is no way to commit suicide because you have to take care about your pet. (Doheny, 2012)

Another hormone, cortisol, serves to strengthen the bonding experience. It functions to mitigate stress by reducing blood pressure, among other things. Oxytocin is considered to benefit mental health and its ability to reduce stress and anxiety. But ironically there is evidence of the ability of oxytocin to also trigger anxiety in humans. In times of social defeat or trauma this hormone appears to target a specific area of the brain that reinforces fear-based memories. Thus, oxytocin can also be responsible for long lasting psychological pain, including memories of a break up.

> The results of this study may explain why certain undesirable memories don't fade, for example in anxiety and PTSP suffers. If a person remembering a terrifying event has a high stress hormone level, the memory of that specific event will be strongly reconsolidated after each retrieval. So, Wolf of the International Graduate School of Neuroscience of Bochum. (Bergland, 2015; Jovasevic et al., 2013)

This research demonstrates not only the impact of animals in therapy for patients suffering from, for example post-traumatic stress, but may be used to aid animals who suffer from separation anxiety. Both human and animals are profiting from these findings.

Early on in our research, it became clear that the combination of animal therapy and psychotherapy resulted in more effective treatments of patients and therapists interviewed. Words to describe the effects included "joy," "liberation," and "hope." Hospitals throughout the United States, Germany, Austria, Switzerland, and the United Kingdom value animal therapy, acknowledging their ability to ease communication between patients and staff, lower patents' feelings of loneliness, and to bring humor into an otherwise serious situation. According to an interview with one nurse, who is working in one of the largest trauma centers in Germany (Hamburg Eppendorf), regular visits with therapy dogs allowed patients suffering from severe pain to reduce medication.

Participating in and observing Pet Therapy in hospitals, rehab-centers, hospice programs, and retirement homes allowed us to witness the positive effects of touch on the residents. Humans crave touch, especially as we find ourselves working alone in cubicles and offices, in front of computers, devoid of positive physical contact with others. One outcome of this need is the popularity of businesses that offer touch, including spas, the massage industry, and other treatments involving touch. While tenderness may be exchanged in the most immediate family, single people barely find ways to satisfy this need. Given this need, pets offer a solution. Companion animals offer unmitigated opportunities for humans to touch, without strings attached, simple and pure.

Furthermore, because modern lives can over-schedule, companion animals offer a solution to the burden by forcing us to break and think beyond our work. An example of one such solution was explored in chapter 2, in which we discussed Japan's creative businesses that cater to the animal-loving professional. Similar businesses are now opening in the United States as animals can help humans to feel calm, escape from the everyday stressors, and achieve a state of mindfulness. Indeed, mindfulness is yet another way to achieve a sense of well-being. Our pets help us to abandon multitasking and to live in the moment.

Nommensen is a strong advocate of mindfully interacting with companion animals, of focusing on the animal when communicating or working with him or her. It is impossible to reap benefits or achieve results in training without focusing on the here and now as animals learn one step at a time. Multitasking only brings confusion to our relationship, and at times, unwanted outcomes.

The ability to focus on the animal and to come up with mutually beneficial ways to interact with pets causes us to be creative and often playful. Much like our children, our pets beckon us to play and move. Likewise, our companion dogs exhibit playfulness, unlike wolves, in intensity. For both wolves and dogs, play is a means to an end, teaching appropriate social and hunting skills to pups: "*Animals that play together tend to stay together*" (Bekhoff, 1972, in Feddersen-Petersen, 2008, p. 224). Play is an important part of socialization for both wolves and dogs and is an activity that take place at all ages and regardless of status in the pack order. The more advanced the species of animal, the more pronounced the period of curiosity, play and imitation in its development (see Feddersen-Petersen, 2004, p. 269).

Dogs partake in play more intensively and for a longer period of time than do wolves as they mature. This may be due to breeding but also to encouragement and training by humans. The more a person encourages play and trains with play, the more a dog will want to play (Feddersen-Petersen, 2004, p. 293). This leads to companion dogs playing into their senior years and allowing us to lose ourselves in creativity and freedom from the mundane.

HUMAN CONTRIBUTIONS TO ANIMAL WELL-BEING

Feelings of well-being in human-animal relationships are not one-sided. We humans elevate the well-being of our four-legged friends in a variety of ways. Numerous studies have shown that the quality of human-animal interaction affects the well-being of animals. In an effort to improve the livestock industry, there has been a rise in interest by animal ranchers and animal husbandry experts to understand how best to accommodate animals to increase productivity as well as welfare. For example, results from several studies show that positive experiences with humans increase the Heat Shock Protein (HSP), which in turn increases an animal's tolerance of stress factors and disease resistance (Zulkifli, 2013, p. 1). Further research has demonstrated that positive daily experiences with stock people can lead to better productivity in farm animals (p. 7).

The most obvious part we play in nurturing animal well-being is in the care of our animals' health with veterinary services. When adopting a pet, responsible pet owners (often formally) agree to keep them healthy and adapt their lives to the pets' needs in oftentimes the most complicated ways.

Practically everything we find in human medicine can be adapted for the care of animals, from heart valve transplants to hip replacement surgery to individually customized chemotherapy. Such a wealth of possibilities opens up new doors for the veterinary profession and yet, speaking as a veterinarian, we run the risk of wanting too much, too fast. With the help of the newest diagnostic devices we can detect the smallest deviation such as a micro-tumor, which we then immediately remove. Such quick responses can lead to neglecting the patient's health as a whole and begins a medical process only because the new diagnostic materials are available, without consideration for psychological or emotional repercussions. Another story from our observations as told by the veterinarian:

> A patient was brought to the clinic that, without the use of chemotherapy, would not survive long. This particular patient was eleven years old and, for this breed of dog, eleven is considered to be old. It was discussed whether or not chemotherapy, a stressful and lengthy therapy, would be a sensible option. After extensive discussions with the owner it was decided to go ahead with the therapy. I might add here that such therapy involves infusions received at the

practice, for many followed by approximately one week of nausea. This is repeated every six weeks. The treatment to curb the cancer lasted six months. Yes, the dog lived for another two years, but we had to continue chemotherapy after a few months. The upshot: two years of life with one of those years enduring chemotherapy—was it worth it? At the time, I was not so sure. While the owners were happy to have had him longer, I am not certain if the dog felt the same way. Despite the wonderful medical possibilities available to cure illnesses, our choice to proceed is not always the best for the patient. Unfortunately, the question is not one we can ask the patients themselves.

Complicating the decision is the fact that we are making a decision not for some random being, but for a being we consider to be a family member or a partner in life. For humans we tend to do everything possible to keep them alive, so why not for our animals?

Another problem plaguing our conscience is the fact that, in setting ourselves up to be "good pet-owners," we feel obliged to pay and do whatever it takes, no matter the cost. It is up to the veterinarian to advise the owner as clearly and fully as possible. This includes explaining all possible forms of rehabilitation and their costs. As a veterinarian herself, Nommensen has found herself in the position of complying with owners' wishes with which she does not agree 100 percent. This leaves the veterinarian in the predicament of rejecting the client or carrying out the wish of the client. Veterinary studies do not include communication courses to help in the process of advising.

In interviews in Germany it was revealed that few veterinary study programs feel compelled to include communication courses, whereas veterinarians themselves agree that education in interpersonal and intercultural communication would be beneficial. Veterinarians interviewed complained about their lack of preparation in working with clients.

Veterinary medicine for small and companion animals is a relatively new and developing field which, unlike other veterinary practices, needs to recognize the complex bond owners have with their pets. Until the mid-twentieth century, veterinarians were mostly concerned with farm animals and treated smaller animals only on the side. Changes in agriculture led to the development of larger farms with over 1,000 animals as opposed to smaller farms of under twenty animals. Veterinarian medicine also advanced with more specialized training for doctors to focus on one species as opposed to many, the latter having been a necessity for smaller farms that were more diverse in animal husbandry. At the same time, small animal husbandry and pet ownership grew. Veterinarians began specializing in small versus large animals and reptiles.

A contemporary model of animal care involves the concept of a center that can harbor numerous specialists in one building, as in a human hospital. In Germany, such centers are found in large urban areas offering numerous benefits. Until recently, small veterinary clinics could not take patients overnight. With the center, a patient can be hospitalized with every necessary technology on hand including large digital x-ray machines and CT scanners, which are too expensive for smaller veterinary operations. The benefit is, as in human medical care, accessibility, less stress due to travel and the ability for referrals to happen in-house. That being said, while advances in physical healthcare for animals over the past fifty years have improved dramatically, our understanding of animal well-being has not kept pace.

Beyond Western medical care, businesses and new therapies have expanded to improve the health of animals. The most obvious examples here include the pet food industry, therapies including acupuncture, massage therapy, and water/swim therapy, behavioral modification programs, indoor exercise equipment, and the dog hotel industry, to mention a few. Hobby enthusiasts help the mental and physical fitness of both their dog and themselves by competing in sports events such as agility, frisbee, tracking, and the like. According to the American Pet Association (2013), "two out of three Americans live with animals, spending more than 55 billion dollars annually on pet welfare."

The question remains: To what extent do these pet industries actually increase the well-being of animals and humans? According to a small experiment Nommensen conducted, the question remains. She is not convinced of the benefits for the animal:

> Having visited numerous animal conventions over the years, I have collected a wealth of products. Which of these do I need? Which of these do I use? After spreading everything out, I picked up what I use on a daily basis. It all fit in my hands. (Nommensen, 2016)

Granted, each pet owner has different needs such that some will require more products than others to enhance their partnership with their pet. Still, the pet industry, like fashion and other industries, have mastered the art of advertising and selling to consumers by creating demand for products.

Even on a basic level a pet does have needs beyond food, water, and shelter. For the dog, it involves regular exercise involving time for socializing and free movement. With more studies being conducted by animal behaviorists, it is clear that free contact in which to develop kinesics, that is, body language, is essential for the full development of a dog's potential. Dogs that are not exposed to such socialization forget how to communicate with other dogs, which leads to leash aggression and extends to aggression, in general, toward humans and other animals. As with humans, lack of socialization with one's own species leads to a lack of mutual understanding, inability to interact appropriately, and fear of others.

During her years working as an animal behaviorist, Nommensen is continuously confronted with answering the question of how much is enough socialization and exercise. The answer is individual, as each breed, each animal, has different requirements: "No matter what the answer, clients are mostly surprised at the amount I prescribe. I am a firm believer that most behavioral problems stem from not enough mental, physical and social stimulation" (Nommensen, 2016).

As previously mentioned, lack of socialization and activity is becoming more of an issue as pets become popular globally in metropolitan and suburban areas. Even the dog that is kept in a yard is lacking in learning how to interact, how to experience and compute new smells, and, as social animals, are deprived of a most basic need: a pack.

Yet, physical exercise and socialization are only part of the requirement for a balanced animal. It is essential that a companion animal is given the opportunity to work mentally on a daily basis and it is up to the pet owner to discover the way forward in stimulating the animal's mind. Animals that do not receive such stimulation may well figure out on their own how to entertain themselves. Here is a story from our observations:

> A colleague had owned her border collie, Jenna, for many years. Jenna was extremely active and was fortunate to accompany my colleague to work each day. But as in any clinic, some days were too stressful to devote enough attention to her, and so Jenna would come up with solutions: she had taken plants in the waiting room from one planter and transferred them to others, with roots and all, gardening in her own fashion, so to speak, much to the amusement of the clients. From then on, whenever she was bored, replanting the plants became her passion. Fortunately, the staff found this behavior tolerable. Left to her own devises however, a pet's solution is not always appreciated.

HUMAN INTERPRETATIONS OF
ETHICAL TREATMENT OF ANIMALS

In examining the relationship between human and animal, it becomes evident that we base the quality of interactions on whether or not the animal lives in our house. When we discuss the animals in our homes, we often talk about them much like we might about a human. We feel connected to them. Farmers, on the other hand, use fewer emotive and emotional vocabulary in discussing their animals. The connection to livestock tends to be described with more ambivalence and in a dismissive, matter-of-fact manner. As we begin to analyze why some animals are chosen as livestock and food whereas others are not, we find ourselves in the middle of the field of animal ethics.

Animal ethics is a field that ponders the extent to which we are morally obligated toward proper and even equal treatment of animals. We mention it here only because it is a growing field, one that is culturally grounded. Animal ethicist, Peter Singer (1994, 1996), examines the history and significance of such analysis as we incorporate animals into our lives, at once as partners and as food.

Animal ethics is a field that has developed over the past one hundred years and in particular since World War II with a rise in farm industry in the United States and parts of Europe. The field is mostly addressed in societies that can afford such questions and in which individuals can survive without animal products. As one colleague stated: "The phenomenon that we suddenly feel a moral obligation toward animals is one that is borne out of luxury. We can afford to consider it because we are not starving" (Nommensen, J., 2017). In such cases the question is asked: Are we treating our animals as we should? The movement has given rise to organic farming, in which animals are allowed to experience the outdoors, graze in pastures, and consume higher quality feed. Farmers in Germany have included toys for their livestock to increase their mental stimulation and well-being. When they can, consumers are willing to pay for this, acknowledging that meat from happy animals tastes better. It remains to be seen how far both industry and consumer will go to assure the well-being of livestock.

Animals that live in our homes have a longer history than farm animals of humans' caring for their well-being. Over time, humans have become more focused on the needs of pets than on those of livestock and today are actively learning how to read their body language, understand pack mentality, and come up with unique ways for their mental stimulation. All this on top of the already acknowledged importance of proper (often debated) feeding and medical care.

Balancing the Human-Animal Relationship: Examples from Training

Because our pets are close to us and share our homes for many years, we engage in a deep bond. In the process of bonding, humans commonly see a reflection of themselves in the animal and thus develop a sense of empathy toward them.

In empathizing on our own terms, we humanize our pets. It is what comes natural to us. It is difficult not to. We adapt our behavior toward our pets as if we were engaging with a new human being, the animal's reaction being interpreted in human terms. As already discussed in more detail in chapter 3, because we analyze in human terms, we are prone to misunderstand our pets. It is here that the animal behaviorist comes into the picture.

Misunderstandings between human and animal can lead to dangerous situations. Most of us feel we know what our pets want when they meow or bark, when they jump up or run in circles, but frequently, interpretations are based on personal feelings rather than scientific observation. For the well-being of both the human and animal, animal signals are significant.

Not only are dogs not human and have dog needs that are different from ours, but dog breeds differ in their needs as well. These differences are ingrained and enduring in their genetic makeup. We see this in puppy play: herding dogs play and make contact with one another differently than hunting breeds. Other breeds, such as terriers, integrate significantly more barking and still others, like sheepdogs—bred for both herding and protection—don't enjoy engaging in play as much as they enjoy patrolling the area and working. It must be added that these are breed-specific tendencies only and individual personalities do vary.

Knowing the basic tendencies and complex characteristics of the breed of my dog helps to understand his qualities and idiosyncrasies, and to expect that certain behaviors are difficult if not impossible to change. Nommensen explains:

> In my practice, a client came to me with her beautiful sheltie, Mia. While a much-loved dog, she had the unnerving tendency during walks with the family to circle them and even bite the ankles of the children. Of course, this is common among herding dogs as they were bred to keep the sheep herds together and moving in a particular direction. However, I agreed that this behavior is challenging and my client need not accept this behavior towards humans. We proceeded to work on obedience training and to motivate her to walk without biting ankles. Her circling continued and the family recognized this to be part of her breed and a characteristic that need not be changed.

Many behaviors that come naturally to breeds can be redirected.

The next story involves a Parson Russell Terrier, Tilda, and exemplifies how redirection can work.

> She was timid around other dogs and rarely engaged in play. What frustrated the owner, Manuela, was her tendency to bark incessantly when another dog approached them. She seemed to be really embarrassed about Tilda's behavior. Nothing she tried seemed to help. I first explained that she, in fact, has a very responsible dog, which sparked her interest. Tilda was not misbehaving, in fact, she had a strong sense of personal space, approximately a one meter radius surrounding her and Manuela, in which she felt safe. When she was uncertain, she would retreat to this space. Other dogs daring to enter this space did not read Tilda correctly forcing her to try and chase them away. Our work proceeded to focus on alternative ways for Tilda to deal with intruders. She learned to lie down next to Manuela, in a relaxed state, rather than to lunge and bark. Understanding the motivation behind behaviors can help a trainer to redirect unwanted behaviors thereby strengthening the relationship of the owner and dog. Manuela was now able to enjoy visiting a dog park for the first time. This was her first step—one in many—for a better understanding and a

closer relationship with her dog. Tilda built up more confidence and was able to face situations more relaxed than before. (Nommensen)

Pet owners have a tendency to gain much happiness from spoiling their companion animals, at times focusing too much on what they as people want for their dogs or, in the other extreme, what their dog wants. What we forget is that mutual benefits are best achieved when the human and her companion animal work as a team. Team work that is stimulating is the best method to achieving long-term positive results for both.

Because dogs live in the moment and are always consciously present, the human part of the team needs to be mindful as well. Dogs do not need continuous attention, but the attention they receive from us as in during training, requires a training partner, the owner, to be present both physically and mentally. Dog parks, for example, work when the human-dog teams are engaged and involved, reading their dogs, and the humans understand that part of their job is to ensure safety while having fun. As mentioned above, multitasking is not recommended.

Beyond the breed, it is important to recognize that animals go through several stages of development beginning at four weeks of age and extending to adulthood, around the age of three, depending on the breed (Feddersen-Petersen, 2004). It is during the early developmental phase that intensive learning takes place, which implies that their ability to take in all experiences and process them is extremely high. Scary events are scarier when they happen to a puppy than when they happen to an adult dog and are therefore harder to overcome later on. Early socialization without overstimulation is essential for a balanced adult animal.

A balanced pet or therapy animal is dependent on a balanced mother, especially in the first 8–12 weeks. A mother that is unbalanced may negatively affect her young. A stressed and fearful mother will likely have stressed and fearful pups. Other patterns of behavior, such as aggression, may also be transferred at an early age. Work by Thompson (et al., 1982) have demonstrated that pregnant dogs exposed to stressful situations are more likely to give birth to nervous puppies (in Feddersen-Petersen, 2004). Knowledge about the period of pregnancy including unexpected events can offer information as to the potential of the puppies.

Nommensen attests to the fact that a minority of her clients and research subjects have concrete knowledge about the developmental phases of dogs leading to a lack of understanding of the learning phases. That being said, these same subjects distinctly remember when their dog hit puberty (between 6–9 months) and again around the second year of life, the "terrible twos." It is a time when suddenly a dog seems to forget all commands she has learned and questions everything you ask of her. Runners, cyclists, or people going for a walk who seem to suddenly appear out of nowhere, can evoke a chase or a fearful response in a dog. It is considered normal behavior, a developmental phase each dog and owner must endure. Again, the ability as an owner and handler to be present and mindful of this phase is necessary. If done with sensitivity, the relationship will flourish.

Both human and animal profit from the human's ability to understand the life phases of their pets. Even the smallest recognition and adjustment can lead to significant positive results. Here is another story from a behaviorist's perspective:

> Over my years helping owners to find a balance in their relationship with their pets, I commonly come across dogs who have forgotten how to be a dog and have resorted to aggression when surrounded by their species. So, it was with Lexie, a gorgeous two-year-old German Shepherd who could not be trusted to play with other dogs. She seemed to think that normal play was tantamount to aggression. She thus preferred to police the dog park and to stop all play sessions from occurring. Because of her age however, she was unable to control her enthusiasm for stopping play and other dogs were hurt. I noted her signals directed at her owner, as if to ask whether she was acting appropriately. The owner was unaware of these signals and so Lexie took it upon herself to judge, alone, without her team partner. Our work together ensued and we worked on the handler reading Lexie's signals (body language). Lexie's behavior improved and today is a wonderful teacher of correct behavior of other young dogs. Lexie's owner continues to inform me that family life has improved as well with Lexie allowing the human to take the lead and tell her when it is appropriate to get involved, to protect or to engage in any way. Her territorial behavior in the house began to decrease—outside in the garden as well. She is able to stay calm and in place on her bed when visitors come in the house or garden. She also gave up following with nipping and controlling the owner all day. At the end of our training the owner told me that at the beginning, he was ready to put her back in a shelter because he felt insecure and helpless with Lexie. His biggest fear that she could turn out aggressive could be prevented. So, at the end there was a good option that both could stay together and benefit the joy from each other.

Another story that shows how important building a good relationship for both sides can be is the story of one of my (Nommensen's) own dogs: dog owners who choose to rescue their dog can attest to how the impact of previous experiences affect their pet. Certain events can trigger the opening of Pandora's box and one can never be certain which events will expose difficult behaviors. Foster parents of such dogs are often keen observers. Nommensen explains:

> Thora came to me from a kill shelter in Hungary. I had driven to get her and brought her home myself. By the time we got home it was night and I attempted to take her out of the car. I assumed she would be thrilled to have been rescued and would jump gleefully out of the car. Well, I was wrong. She

refused to come out and even growled. There I stood, with an open door, the behaviorist who should know better and yet, I could not even approach my own dog. After a few moments, I remembered the words of the caretaker at the shelter, that Thora knew the command for come. I whistled and out she jumped, without a problem. She was seemingly surprised at her own response she stared at me and decided to trust me from then on. It was a magical moment between the two of us but our work together had only begun . . .

Thora and I began training for search and rescue when she was two. While she learned quickly I needed more training. Complicating things, I figured Thora understood this about me and seemed to be working two jobs: finding the injured person as quickly as possible and ensuring that I was not getting lost in the woods. The latter job resulted in her rarely leaving my side.

She blossomed in all other aspects of her work, but we soon discovered that she feared men. Especially men in working dress (overalls). We first caught wind of this problem at our own home, when a neighbor (wearing blue overalls) dared to ride his bike past our house. Thora escaped our yard and took to the chase. No one was hurt, but we had been warned and something had to be done. From then on, we used more men as our "victims" in search and rescue training. Thora had to learn to separate from me as this is part of what we do in search and rescue: the dogs searches, finds and then alerts us that a victim has been found. I, as the other part of the team, needed to feel certain that she would do her job well without further victimizing the victim. We had to build up trust. So we both had to grow in this relationship. I must say she taught me a lot about what it takes to build a healthy working relationship. I even used my experience with her in how I developed my relationship with my children, through trust. It took a year, but in the end, she qualified and we were a skillful team who had learned to work together and to trust each other, giving each other a sense of security and calm. (Nommensen)

That a relationship with animals can even aid the development of self-understanding is exemplified in the story of Emmi, a Podenco Canario hound, and her person. She had been rescued in Malaga and was healing from a leg fracture.

Emmi came to us in pain, afraid and undernourished. The first days in our hospital were stressful and she bit everyone who came near her. With much care and patience, she learned to trust our hands. Once released, the owner continued tirelessly to work with her and after a year, the dog became a friendly, outgoing companion. However, it was not only the dog who benefitted from the experience. When she arrived with the dog, she was a quiet and shy person and the staff jokingly noted that both animal and human were similar. Through Emmi's socialization process, the owner also learned to become more confident by attending various training programs. In a communication, she wrote: "Emmi has taught me much about life. Together we overcame all her problems and I grew. The experience gave me the courage to open my own sewing business. I am so proud of us both." (M. Janina, 2016)

Working as a team with our pets can lead to unforeseen positive emotional outcomes.

It remains essential that, as we intertwine our human lives with that of our pets', we recognize the animal as animal, the dog as dog. Everything we do is processed by our dogs as only a dog would compute. She is continuously aware of our behaviors, reading us and expecting us to do the same for her. This requires that we control our body, become mindful and learn to react quickly and efficiently as leaders, but also as part of a team. As mindful, present partners we enhance each other's daily lives and sense of well-being.

CONCLUSION

In this chapter, the authors reflect on how animals and humans benefit each other through their intimate connections. Throughout our research, we were impressed by the extent to which humans are enriched by pets and therapy animals. Our hypothesis had been that both humans and animals benefit equally. Instead, we found that in all likelihood, humans have much more to gain as animals can influence and even alter a person's life in distinct and positive ways. Those we interviewed supplied us with stories, some of which we included, that demonstrate the depth of impact animals can have on personal lives including diminishing recuperation periods, strengthening of the immune system, increasing fitness levels, and enhancing physical capabilities as well as boosting self-confidence, self-awareness, and mindfulness. Even with an education in veterinary sciences and animal behaviorist, Nommensen was surprised to find the extent to which animals impact the lives of humans. Granted, the focus for Nommensen has been mainly on animals in training and therapy and the resulting changes in their behavior. That their presence can alter behavior patterns of humans so effectively was a revelation. In fact, the stories we have collected in all likelihood merely scrape the surface of the extent to which animals can positively impact human lives.

Chapter Five

The Animal's Perspective

Up until now, this book has focused on ways in which companion animals have contributed to human well-being. We concluded that cohabitation and working with animals in certain societies can enrich the lives of humans. Perhaps the readers can attest to this with their personal experiences as well. However, to what extent are we interacting appropriately with our compatriots? In this chapter, Nommensen, challenges our presumptions about animals and asks us to abandon our limiting human-centric perspective. Nommensen focuses on the perspective of dogs, as these are the animals we engage most frequently as service animals. The author addresses whether our interpretations of animal behavior are adequate for reinforcing mutually beneficial experiences and how we can work as an effective team with our canine companions. While there is much scholarship on how dogs and other animals think, this chapter is geared specifically to ensure the mutually beneficial relationship between humans and working animals in service and therapy. By starting with understanding how animals perceive their environment and ending with best practices in handling animals, this chapter offers solutions to enable a supportive working relationship between humans and animals.

As discussed in chapter 3, pack animals evolved to quickly and appropriately read and respond to body language in order to survive as a member of that pack, herd, or family. They are adaptable and can easily live closely with other species, learn their patterns of behavior, and kinesics. Dogs, horses, and cats have been known to read human emotions accurately due to their ability to sense and even smell changes in our body odor as we switch moods. However, while animals can indeed sense our emotional state, they are not intellectually driven to discover why a person feels the way she does. Rather, a companion, service, or therapy animal simply knows that a person feels a certain way at that particular moment. Whereas to humans the reasons and the contexts in which we feel a certain way matter, dogs to not ponder the cause of emotions. Experts in mindfulness, animals perceive and only care about what is going on now. It is the moment that matters, not the history. Working with animals raises our awareness of the present.

CANINE SENSE OF IDENTITY

Human and non-human animals differ in their perceptions of their environment in significant ways. Deciding factors contributing to the use of an animal's senses depends on the strength of each one. In humans, the strongest sense is vision, whereas in rats, cats, and dogs, the nose rules. Cats are unique in that they have a stronger ability to capture optically at dusk than humans, dogs, and rats. We humans are more likely to find the red ball than the perfumed, green cloth in a green field. A dog senses the opposite of what we sense in this instance.

And so, because of his keen nose, a dog develops a sense not just of other objects, but of his place in the environment through impressions gained mainly from scent. This happens immediately after birth: while all senses develop as an animal grows up, very early, with eyes still closed, puppies and kittens recognize themselves not only as members of a species, but as belonging to a family by scent:

> kittens with their eyes still closed have been known to hiss at the presence of a cat other than their mother just as puppies with their eyes still closed have been known to growl at the presence of a scent of a dog other than their mothers. (Albrecht, 2008, p. 58)

Each individual animal, including the human, has his own unique scent, which animals detect and register at birth, leading to the ability to distinguish family from not family.

A puppy is born blind and deaf, but her sense of smell is already developed enough so that she can discriminate her mother from other dogs, and even more specifically, which nipple is designated for her. The nose is thus the primary organ that helps a dog makes sense of her surroundings and facilitates survival. It is the one that is most developed and ready to work the earliest. Ears and eyes develop two weeks later.[1] Interestingly, the sense of smell is also the first organ to develop in humans: while we can distinguish between scents, our ability to see and hear are significantly less developed at birth. That being said, sight and hearing overpower the capacity to smell as the human baby grows.[2]

Because of our bias for vision, humans are often taken aback that dogs do not perceive things we find obvious, such as an orange object on a green field. Dogs do not use their eyes in the same way humans do. With a wider visual capacity of approximately 240 degrees as compared with that of a human at 200 degrees, dogs have a reduced capacity to utilize both eyes simultaneously in a 60-degree radius. Humans can do so in 120 degrees. This results in a reduced ability to focus on details for dogs. Instead, the dog's nose is the organ that detects the details while the eyes come into play at shorter distances when the nose has done all it can. Colors are of less importance to dogs than what they can smell, and indeed, the range of scent possibilities offers more information than a color.

Dogs only have cones in the retina to perceive blue and green tones. Hues of red, including orange, do not stand out. Moreover, dogs suffer from astigmatism with the cornea focusing at a range of 2–4 diopters in contrast to 15 diopters for humans. At a distance of 30–50 centimeters, objects begin to appear blurry for dogs. You will notice dogs raising their noses and to sniff out what appears far away before focusing with their eyes.[3]

PRIORITIZATION OF SENSES AND THE IMPACT ON WORKING WITH DOGS

Over the years of working with dogs and educating humans, Nommensen has confirmed that dogs, when possible, prioritize their senses with smell being most important, followed by sight, then hearing, then voice, then touch. Humans, on the other hand, when possible, tend to prioritize sight, then hearing, followed by voice, touch, and smell. Because we, as humans, tend to prioritize the senses differently than dogs, we are tempted to utilize what comes naturally to us in training others, including animals, by focusing on verbal commands (voice) and gestures (sight) without entertaining the use of senses that work best for animals. One exception is training for tracking lost people and animals. In this training, the handler does not speak or name the desired behavior until the dog has figured out on his own what he needs to follow. In this training dogs are taught to learn through their noses. Only once the dog has the understanding of our expectations do we name the activity and offer a command.

> My Search and Rescue dog, Scipio, never ceases to surprise me. On his second real track, he seemed to have caught the scent of the lost dog. He took me down a street and up onto a porch then to the center of a front lawn. There he stood, panting, ears perked, looking at me as if to say: "Now what?" I despaired. Obviously, he had forgotten what he was supposed to do, I thought. I tried to send him on. He did not go. I told the sad owners that he had lost the scent. That perhaps the dog had been picked up at that spot. Days later a call came in and indeed, the spot at which we had stood in despair was the spot at which a lady had picked up the little dog she had presumed needed rescuing. The dog was returned well fed and pampered. (Fujimura)

To dogs, scent paints an image and tells a story with nuances and answers to more than just where an individual went, who it was, with whom she went, and even how the individual felt at the time. Search dogs trained to track criminals are trained to pick up not only human scent but scent that indicates stress which is most likely emitted when a criminal is on the run. Other scent molecules that are detected as part of an individual's scent include shampoo used, food eaten, lotions, and the like. Both genetics and the environment make up an individual's unique scent (Albrecht, p. 59).

The importance of smell is evidenced in how animals greet each other. In an initial meeting humans connect with their eyes, which may be followed by a handshake or even a hug, reducing distance between each other fairly quickly. Dogs on the other hand, approach each other indirectly, from a distance, followed by circling and yes, smelling each other indiscreetly. They read each other including each other's gender, rank, emotions, and energy, and accordingly they decide to move closer to or move away from one another. According to Nommensen, the manner in which we, as dog owners, greet each other—dogs on leash, straight at each other—presents as unnatural for dogs. This form of greeting needs to be trained so that it is not perceived as threatening, possibly leading to aggression. Most dog owners do not think of training the behaviour as it seems perfectly natural to us, and we are surprised when our dogs react other than peacefully.

The question was asked: If dogs are so dependent on their noses, how do they envision their identity as individuals and indeed, do they have a sense of self at all? As Horowitz asks further, if so, how do they identify it (Horowitz, 2016, p. 23). She discusses the "mirror mark" test used for other mammals in which a face of an animal is marked. In this experiment, it was asked how does an animal react when encountering her own marked face in a mirror?

> By the time a child is eighteen months old, he will reach up to remove a sticker an adult has surreptitiously placed on his head when he sees it in a mirror, thus passing the test. (p. 24)

She adds that animals such as chimpanzees and even an elephant can pass this test. Dogs however, cannot: imagine showing your dog the mirror when his face is covered with stickers. He will, no doubt express indifference (p. 24).

But does this mean a dog has no sense of himself? Horowitz decided to test this by designing an "olfactory mirror," feeling quite confident that dogs perceive first and best through their noses:

> Instead of a reflective surface, we used a canister exuding odour. When you look in the mirror, you smell . . . yourself. When you smell the canister, you smell . . . yourself. I used a dog's own scent as well as a revised "scent image": the scent, altered (or "marked"). We were asking whether the dogs would tell

the difference and whether their marked self would be more interesting to smell. . . . And the result: dogs passed the test. Our subjects spent way more time sniffing their olfactory image when it had been marked, as though looking at the mirror most when there was something funny between their teeth. (p. 28)

Beyond themselves and others, dogs use their olfactory capabilities to know the time of day, a new day, oncoming bad weather, illness, memories and so much more. As Horowitz notes: "there is no such thing as "fresh air" to a dog" (p. 29).

SENSING ENERGY AND THE RUCKSACK EFFECT

Our emotional energy can be misunderstood by animals just like we can misunderstand theirs. When such misunderstandings occur, the relationship is jeopardized. Take for example a situation that occurs countless times a day. A person takes her dog for a walk after a long day at work. The person has low energy and allows the dog to meander on leash in front. Another dog comes around the corner and begins to bark and growls. The handler of this dog scolds him and shortens the leash. The person is surprised and slightly perturbed and, in response, slows down, avoids the other dog and shortens the leash. A dog in this instance will read the handlers insecurity and can easily feel the need to enter protection mode by also growling and barking, possibly even lunging. In an instance, the dog has taken over the person's role as leader in order to ensure his person's safety. The fact that this was not the reaction the person had wanted or envisioned does not make sense to the dog as the person's energy signaled insecurity. Such situations are frequently described in Nommensen's practice. Clients note the seemingly unexpected nature of such situations as they do not see the signaling of their dogs and moreover do not understand the effect their own energy has.

A handler's state of mind is constantly being analyzed by their dog. As mentioned previously, we carry everything we are and feel, like a rucksack on our back. In order to respond effectively to our animals, we need to take it off and be alert to our surroundings, cast grudges and judgments aside and be intellectually present. Below are a few examples from the author's practice:

> Lisa, an animal lover, came to me because her female Whippet, Trini, was showing signs of leash aggression when encountering other dogs on a walk. Trini had been rescued from an animal shelter in Malaga, emaciated and fearful. Lisa worked hard with Trini, feeding her so that she might arrive at a normal weight and taking her to obedience classes, so she could learn to be a good companion to her. I observed who Lisa and Trini responded to in staged dog or human encounters. We found that Trini was the boss on walks, directing the direction, pace and even which dogs could be greeted or not. Trini took

it upon herself to ward off anyone who came too close to Lisa. Lisa resolved this pattern by picking up Trini assuming that Trini was insecure and afraid of the other dogs. Lisa had not forgotten Trini's terrible past and felt the need to rescue her whenever she thought her dog exhibited fear. She still carried the weight of Trini's story in her rucksack. Lisa's response, however, signaled to Trini not that Lisa was protecting her, but that Lisa was insecure and fearful herself. Trini felt compelled to protect Lisa. As soon as Lisa was able to put Trini's past out of her mind, she was better able to analyze the situation objectively, making Trini follow her lead, commands and feel empowered. (Nommensen)

Rather than attribute emotional states to our dogs, we need to learn to read dogs better. We cannot count 100 percent that a dog will act as we think she should act for the reasons we believe to be true. In fact, we often misread the emotional energy of our animals. Working with dogs as an animal behaviorist Nommensen realized that people misread even basic emotions. When asked what a happy dog looks like, the majority of the population studied responded: jumping, running freely, playful, medium to high energy, cuddly, and wagging his tail. Frequently, these descriptors of a happy dog are correct. However, we fail to see that a calm dog, with head low to the ground, walking behind a human can also be happy. Jumping, running wild, cuddling, and tail wagging can be signs of emotions other than happiness. In fact, the more energy enters into play among dogs, the less in control a dog is, which can lead to aggressive interactions.

For many years one of the authors had a dilemma. As the owner of an extremely positive and high energy male Viszla, Neo, she, the animal trainer, would be embarrassed by her dog who felt the need to jump on people. Simply teaching him "no" or "off" or "sit" was not sufficient. He had taken the leadership role from her. Then, after a seminar, she understood: dogs can be followers and can be happy at the same time. In dog families, only few will take the leadership role. The others are not depressed or stressed, rather, they have given the job of leader to the more qualified dogs. Once she took the lead on walks, became calm, and demanded the follower role of Neo, greeting people appropriately became the norm and the jumping stopped. Nommensen became aware of the extent to which emotions can infiltrate the work situation.

In a positive relationship between human and animal, the human's emotions ameliorate the outcome of the job. This is only possible if we also understand which emotions are best suited for which task. Note that people can have a similar effect on each other. If the emotions are genuine, a calm person can have a calming effect on a group of people. Imagine the result of having a group of calm people joined by one excited person . . . it only takes seconds to change everyone's emotions.

MINDFULLY CHALLENGING THE MIND

Rather than conferring humanity onto our pets, it makes sense to offer them opportunities to develop in ways that are meaningful to both human and animal. This requires that we step back from anthropomorphizing and break from the routines we cherish to reinforce a positive relationship. In order for animals to work for us, they must be motivated to do so and find interest in the task. Learning from the authors experience, creating an interesting and stimulating environment for our four-legged partners is the best way to begin.

Animals need breaks in the routine as they enjoy learning and being challenged mentally. Without mental stimulation, the well-being of the pet must be questioned. Even a change in the walk pattern, allowing a dog to carry a light backpack, visiting parks, and stopping in dog friendly shops or the veterinarian to say hi, all these can contribute to an animal's balanced emotional state. Of course, this is easiest in a society that is open to dogs being walked in public spaces and in public venues. In Germany, as in many other European countries, dogs are frequently encountered in restaurants, to which tourists from the United States have been known to comment with surprise at how well behaved the dogs in Germany are. As a result of such dogs being allowed to accompany their owners, physically and mentally stimulated by visiting places, their well-being is improved and expressed by their balanced emotional state and behavior.

During her research in the United States, Nommensen found an overwhelming majority of dog owners to whom a dog walk was an exception, not a rule. Dogs were mostly kept in the house or in the yard. It was precisely these dog owners who had more issues with their dogs' behavior patterns including barking, high energy, or even obsessive-compulsive behaviors, including excessive licking or chewing. To her this was a surprise finding. In Germany, Nommensen found the opposite problem: over-balanced dogs who are alarmed and excited by very little.

As mentioned above, there are the overworked dogs. Just as with humans, a dog has his limits in working capacity and needs time to regain energy. While exercise and mental stimulation lead to an emotionally balanced dog, too much work can lead to mental (and physical) fatigue and stress. In our work in search and rescue, both authors know well the importance of taking breaks including long sleep breaks. Search and rescue teams attest to the fact that in these moments of resting, an animal recaptures and stores the day's events, including the mistakes made during training and work evidenced in their behaviour, often self-corrected upon awakening.

As with humans, animals experience sleep cycles that are structured by stages: stage 1, a stage between wakefulness and sleep, often referred to as somnolence; stage 2, light sleep; stage 3, deep sleep or slow—wave sleep and rapid eye movement (REM) sleep. New experiences and abilities are deposited in all mammals in the hippocampus during deep sleep, which can be measured by an increase in a hormone level, that of noradrenaline. Noradrenaline enables new experiences to be stored in the brain.

Psychologist Kenway and his colleagues studied this phenomenon in rats and found that during both awake time and deep sleep, EEG patterns were similar. They concluded that rats were reliving the experience of running through a labyrinth in their sleep. During disrupted sleep, the stress hormone, cortisol, increases and does not decrease during periods of rest. As a result, memory is weakened, as is the ability to concentrate and the immune system is compromised (Kenway, 2001; Susan, 2000; Walker and Stickgold, 2004).

THE ANIMAL AS INDIVIDUAL

As we employ animals for service, therapy, or simply as companions, we often fail to see them as individuals. Certainly, the breed of dog or cat is an important factor when choosing an animal for a job, but the fact remains that within a breed, the variation of personality types is large. Each breed provides "low," "medium," or "high" energy characters. So we have to take a closer look at individuals and step back from thinking in stereotypes.

In Nommensen's practice, she frequently meets families who express their desire for less excitable dogs. A common lament: "We wanted a calm family dog and so we chose a Golden Retriever, but ours just isn't like the others." Indeed, Goldens can be calm . . . or not. Dachshunds can be hard to train . . . or not. A Belgian Malinois can be bold . . . or not. Choosing the appropriate dog for a job goes well beyond the breed. This understanding of animals is essential to ensuring not only the success of the task at hand, but to enhance the selected animal's well-being as well. Animals on the wrong job can lose trust in people, become anxious, aggressive, and even depressed.

For example, in search and rescue, it is essential that the right dog for the job is chosen, one that is curious, driven, but also emotionally balanced at work. Matching the human with a dog of similar temperament leads to even more positive outcomes. When this is not the case, the relationship can be molded to lead to a collegial and beneficial working relationship. In the case of Nommensen, she has a dog, Neo, that is highly energetic. She, on the other hand, describes herself as a more of a medium energy person. Before they actually work, Neo needs to exercise, to let off steam, so that they match in energy levels and both can focus. Were they to start work without exercise, they would both be frustrated with each other and effective searching could not be accomplished.

Many dog owners come to Nommensen convinced that their dog refuses to work with them. However, one of the most important characteristics of dogs is their pack mentality and their desire to work with the others to enhance their ability to thrive. They are motivated to please. Dogs described as unwilling or stubborn are frequently stressed due to their high energy levels making them unable to concentrate on the owner's demands. Refusal to cooperate is also a sign that communication between human and animal is lacking.

Therapy animals need the same preparation for work as do service animals. Depending on the individual animal, without exercise first, being touched can trigger excitement rather than calm energy, the latter being preferable when working with elderly or ailing individuals. Even a small breed needs to be calm when, for example, being read to by a child in the PAWS for Reading program in which this author is involved. Teaching the author's teammate, Rosie, a miniature Dachshund, to lay calmly beside a child who is excitedly reading to her was no small task. A good long walk beforehand works wonders. Balance is key to effectively engaging working dogs.

In extreme cases, animals are born with imbalances that lead to behavioral problems. Just like humans can struggle to be balanced and may be diagnosed with phobias, so can animals. We often assume the animal exhibits phobic behaviors because of former negative experiences, and while this can certainly be true, animals can simply be wired a certain way. Just as with humans, therapy for the animal can be helpful. A client appeared with such a case:

> A family dog, a one-year-old Dalmatian they had acquired as a puppy, showed extreme anxiety the minute she would go outdoors. At home, she appeared to be well-balanced. Once on the sidewalk, she would become catatonic, shiver, drool and urinate. Every noise spooked her. Walks became a chore but the owners persisted and figured "she is just mentally slow to learn." I suggested therapy that cost time and money. They were not able to agree due to financial challenges and a lack of time. After much discussion, they decided to give the Dalmatian to a family that had time to dedicate to the rehabilitation of the dog. Moreover, this new family had four calm dogs who were able to teach her how to be part of a pack in which the calmer, more experienced dogs became role models with behaviors easily imitated by the Dalmatian. We worked slowly but surely to help her manage her fear of noises among her new kin. The result: she became a relaxed representative of her breed. (Nommensen)

Sometimes we need to step back and decide what is best for all. Taking the dog away from its owners was hard, but both parties benefitted from that decision. As it turned out, the original owners of the dog got along better with cats, finding them less stressful, less work, more independent. The dog integrated into his new family as a full pack member, and her confidence increased and her fear of noises disappeared.

To summarize, we can conclude that for an animal and human to work well together, to mutually benefit from each other's presence, to work as a team, it is imperative that certain factors are considered:

1. Is this the ideal job for the two of us? Does the human have realistic expectations?
2. Are we both emotionally balanced and responsive to each other in a positive way?
3. Do we have the proper training skills in place to become an effective team?
4. Are we willing to treat the animal as a team member and ensure the animal's well-being?

Without these considerations, benefits are unlikely.

As we come to understand the gifts animals can bring us, they awaken in us the feeling of love and being loved, giving and receiving empathy, self-worthiness, and capable. Through their ability to adapt to our human lives, they have entered our families and workplaces to the point of no return. They will continue to act as our working partners, teammates and family members. It is up to us to ensure their well-being.

CONCLUSION

In this chapter, we have attempted to bring the world of dogs closer to you. While the fact that humans and animals perceive their surroundings differently is no secret, few authors (with the exception of Horowitz, 2016; Warren, 2013, and a few others) delve into the senses of the dogs, in particular their sense of smell, when discussing training. Without such insight, the worlds we inhabit remain incomprehensible. Dogs prioritize their senses, with the sense of smell being the most significant. It is therefore not surprising that their picture (indeed an awkward term as they are not primarily visual creatures) of the world and responses to it vary from ours. Furthermore, as we have seen in previous chapters, pack animals are artists of body language, desiring harmony even with certain unknown species and for our purposes, with humans. Because of dogs' great adaptability to our world, humans often fail to understand and recognize the small alarm signals (body language) that are given by their dogs. For us, problems often appear in a very late stage. Dogs do not possess "bad tempers," nor do they act behind our backs. Rather, dogs communicate with their environment 24/7, sending and responding with signals through body language. Each signal that an animal sends represents a reflection of their relationship to the other. Their signals present an opportunity for us to responsibly seek more subtle readings of them and to acknowledge that dogs are not trying to deceive or otherwise inhibit communication or as Nommensen describes in her native language: "aufhoeren den schwarzen Peter den Hunden zuzuschieben und somit unsere Verantwortung an dieser Situation abzugeben (to cease blaming the dog for unwanted behaviors and with that relinquishing our responsibility of the situation)."

This chapter illuminates problems in our training methods and underscores the fact that interspecies communication between humans and other animals, as exemplified in how we interact with dogs, remains human-centric. Research for this book has shown that the tendency to consider the animals' perspectives and body language in dog training for companionship is more pronounced in Germany than in the United States. Utilizing methods in training that also answer the needs and signals of dogs is widespread and normalized in Germany. Behaviorist and ethologist Guenter Bloch (Hundefarm-Eifel, Bad Muenstereifel) and Dr. Dorit Feddersen-Petersen (student of Konrad Lorenz at the University Kiel) began their early discoveries (1977) of canine and wolf behavior and communication. Their research on animal body language remains foundational for European behaviorists, trainers, and animal psychologists. Beginning in 2000, the study of animal behavior in Germany blossomed, significantly altering methods to canine-centered training for companion dogs, search and rescue, police work, and other canine services. Dog owners across Germany are educated intensively on canine kinesics and on effective and humane responses to animal communication. Even in kennels and animal control institutions, workers are made aware of the significance of pack mentality and to read the way in which dogs interact with one another. In these programs, staff have come to learn how canine-centric communication with dogs allows for better quality of life for them: dogs in kennels, when treated thusly tend to be calmer, more balanced, and with fewer behavior problems. Nommensen discovered, much to her surprise, throughout her research for this book that in the United States not all dog training organizations embrace the importance of the canine perspectives and body language in their training. She writes in her findings: "I had assumed that the United States would be ahead on this subject but was mistaken. Rather a degree of anthropomorphizing the dog, which can easily lead to miscommunication, is still common" (2017). The importance of animal perceptions cannot be stressed enough. Disseminating the importance of kinesics and the senses in training globally would enhance the experience for both human and canine. In order to fully do justice to, to understand and explain the complexity of animal senses, how their unique ways of taking in the world around them, how their perceptions enrich their comprehension and "vision" of their environment, and how, in turn, these are communicated, would lead to an entirely new manuscript.

NOTES

1. http://www.hundewissen-bremen.de, http://www.welpen.de, and http://www.pedigree. de. Accessed May 21, 2017.

2. http://www.familie.de/baby/fuenf-sinne-beim-baby-510887.html. Accessed May 21, 2017.

3. http://www.dogssunshine.de/rund/lexikon/hunde-sehen-anders-als-menschen.html. Accessed May 21, 2017.

Concluding Remarks

At the start of this book project, we, the authors, were confident that our combined knowledge in animal psychology, anthropology and veterinary medicine would suffice for a commentary on any research we might conduct. We soon realized that our research went beyond confirming our hypotheses, rather, causing us to ask more questions about the complexity of human-animal relations in diverse cultural contexts. We now understand that this book, rather than merely providing insights, is a springboard for further studies: it barely scratches the surface on the subject of well-being as it is enhanced by our companion, therapy, and service animals. We hope that this book has inspired further curiosity in our readers, as it has in us. The extent to which animals enhance our well-being is substantial and carries much potential for therapeutic programs.

One phenomenon which caught our attention was the extent to which humans, be they keen observers of wild animals, personal owners, or professionals, working with service and therapy animals are preoccupied with contemplating and utilizing animals as positive contributors to their lives. As topics of thought, media, literature, and conversation, animals are a unifying force. They connect us to each other, regardless of social status, income, education, and background.

Our relationship with animals and our moral outlook on them is, to a large extent, dependent on our spiritual and religious belief systems, as evidenced in the societies we studied.

This book began with an overview of the complex social history in England, Germany, and the United States, that led to the acceptance of animals in our homes as protectors, as pets, as companions, and as healers. We discussed the types of therapy animals provide beyond the obvious work they do for humans with special needs. Our discussions show that as society changed, so did attitudes toward animals, ultimately leading to our acceptance of certain animals as powerful and significant enhancers of human lives. Via this realization, we conclude that humans need to embrace the next level of our relationship, which is to ensure the ethical treatment of animals as we use them to our advantage. We advocate a partnership rather than a one-sided relationship.

What brings a society to the point that its members can consider ethical treatment of animals has everything to do with cultural heritage. Different cultures have different perspectives on the human-animal bond which depend on its ethos, the emotional community that determines outlook and key interests. Perspectives and definitions, sometimes subconscious, develop over time and undergo continuous change. We witness such differences and changes as we study religions and spirituality as foundations of the treatment and use of animals beyond Germany and the United States, to include Russia and Japan. One similarity among these traditions is the notion of dominion over animals, which has slowed the process of ethical treatment of working animals and even pets, as people at once incorporate them into their families while simultaneously treating them as material possessions.

By both anthropomorphizing and objectifying companion animals and service animals, what appears as communicating and relating to animals may in fact be miscommunicating affecting well-being of humans and animals in, at times, problematic ways. Well-being for both human and animal can be compromised.

Well-being is a concept that evolved out of the field of positive psychology, "the scientific study of the strengths that enable individuals and communities to thrive. The field is founded on the belief that people want to lead meaningful and fulfilling lives, to cultivate what is best within themselves, and to enhance their experiences of love, work and play" (The Positive Psychology Center, 2017). While the term was created by Maslow in 1954, the idea was not academically and practically developed until the late 1990s. Today the philosophy behind positive psychology has gone beyond the limits of the medical field and its fundamental goal of enhancing human well-being has formed the basis for the development, production, and marketing of numerous organizations. Many industries such as community services, educational programs, museums, housing developments, and businesses market their ability to improve customer well-being. Take for example some of the slogans used by corporations:

Coke: "Open Happiness"
Disneyland: "The Happiest Place on Earth"
General Electric: "We bring good things to life"
L'Oréal: "Because you are worth it"
Whole Foods: "Food from a Happy Place"

According to these businesses, they are manifestations of our happiness that we want to attain and buying their product gets us closer. In the United States, in particular, happiness, a feeling beyond mere contentment, that is connected to good physical and mental health has become a cultural fixation.

If we go further and Google "culture of well-being," the sites claiming to help improve employee well-being in the workplace seem to be endless. Add to these industries the list of self-help media including books, videos, and audio programs, fitness, yoga, and meditation classes, it would appear that Western societies are either truly ill and need extreme intervention or that we have found the way to life-long happiness through the pursuit of buying well-being. Is this simply a luxury found in the West that other societies can ill afford?

Many a citizen's focus on well-being is based on the belief that we need to look beyond what we have, to have more, to feel and have better quality goods in order to experience true well-being. This desire for more has been well studied in psychology, the social sciences, and the business marketing fields. However, a new trend is equally fascinating: the turn to our immediate cultural and personal environments and a realization that we needn't look far to harvest a sense of well-being. Nature, parks, wildlife, and, indeed, the animals we keep, all are venues proven to enhance our lives. As studies confirm, nature can speak to us (Wohlleben, 2016) and can work with us to achieve mutually beneficial goals. Beyond nature, Western societies are afforded the luxury of turning to our non-human companions and engage them as true partners on our journeys through life.

Scientific studies of the benefits of animals to our health have begun, however, the insights gained in qualitative research as an outcome of interviews and participation-observation present unquantifiable data comprised of personal and cultural narratives. As we make our daily rounds in hospice, each person we encounter is in a different place, with a personal history unlike anyone else's. Their reaction to animals, while also culturally determined, is their individual reaction, unique, but as important as anyone else's reaction and experiences. Some interactions will prove more beneficial to patients than others. Some patients, after all, will be more open to the interacting with animals given their life experiences. The leadership at hospice, nevertheless, always welcomes its animal therapy teams with open arms, pushing us to come more often because, in one doctor's words: "I have seen miracles happen when dogs come to visit" (Weiger, 2015). In our studies, we have found that, indeed, in Germany and the United States there is a positive correlation between human health and animal interaction. This may be particular to Western culture and to societies that place animals higher on the totem pole.

Significant to the potential of animals for human well-being is the cultural context surrounding human animal interactions. Cultural beliefs about animals can potentially predict the degree to which an animal can contribute to human well-being in societies. This book will hopefully function as a baseline from which scholars can launch a cross-cultural comparison of the connection between animals and human well-being in a variety of social and cultural settings.

To summarize, we can conclude that humans, in the context of cultures that value animals as potential friends, partners, or family members can benefit in a number of ways including:

- Improved fitness levels as owners and handlers exercise with animals
- A more robust immune system
- Psychological well-being
- Enhanced psychological and physical development and rehabilitation in Animal Assisted Therapy
- Improved social health as pets act as social enablers thus combatting feelings of loneliness and social isolation
- Improved sense of personal capabilities as humans successfully care for an animal (Smith, 2012, pp. 349–442).

Finally, as we work with animals, the question remains as to whether such work is morally justified, or does the concept of working with animals merely mask the reality of use and abuse of animals? While organizations supporting Animal Assisted Therapy insist that animals be humanely treated, protected from stress, and given proper amounts of water, exercise, and rest, the moral implications are more complex and need to be considered (Zamir, 2006, p. 180).

Morally, we need to be aware that in using animals for our well-being, we are limiting their freedom, asking them to behave in response to our needs as we train them, segregate them from their natural peers, expose them to potential harm, and so forth, to name a few limitations we place on our non-human companions. At what point does use become abuse? In answer to this dilemma, we have found that in most cases, human-animal team work can be beneficial for both. This is particularly the case in which animals that have been bred to live with humans are involved. As philosopher Zamir neatly summarizes:

> Forms of AAT (Animal-Assisted Therapy) that rely on horses and dogs are continuous with the welfare of these animals. Without a relationship with humans, an overwhelming number of these beings would not exist. . . . But given responsible human owners, such lives are qualitatively comfortable and safe, and they need not frustrate the social needs of these creatures. A world in which practices like AAT exists is an overall better world for these beings than one that does not include them and this provides a broad, moral vindication of forms of AAT that rely on these beings. On the other hand, rodents, birds,

monkeys, reptiles, and dolphins gain little by coercing them into AAT . . . such forms should be abolished. (Zamir, 2006, p. 195)

Throughout these studies it is difficult to assess who benefits more, animal or person and ultimately, how? How do we measure to what extent an animal benefits from the relationship? What are the yet to be discovered possibilities for animals working in hospice or therapy? Such questions call for more investigation. What we do know is that the full potential for greater health benefits are yet to be ascertained and essential in order to reach people from diverse social strata. We believe firmly that it is in this research that suspected possibilities will come to life.

From working with animals, in particular dogs, it is clear that humans and animals can achieve endless benefits from each other's companionship and teamwork. As we leave from writing today, we are ready to grab our dogs' halters. They will inevitably jump up and run to the door, excited to go on another track, to search for and hopefully save another lost being or to offer a paw to an ailing individual in hospice. They may never have had this job without us, but to be sure, they enjoy it: the anticipation in the car, the actual process of running through fields, nose to the ground, on the hunt, so to speak, the joy we all express that the being (human or pet) has been found, or running to open arms of a person in need, the ultimate reward and the deep sense of contentment as we return home after a job well done.

Bibliography

Akademie für tierärztliche Fortbildung ATF. www.bundestierärztekammer.de. Accessed May 20, 2017.

Albrecht, K. (2008). *Dog Detectives*. Wenatchee, Washington: Dogwise Publishing.

Allen, K., Blascovitch, J., and Mendes, W. B. (2002). Cariovascular reactivity and the presence of pets, friends and spouses: The truth about cats and dogs. *Psychosomatic Medicine*, 64, pp. 727–739.

Allen, K., Blascovitch, J., Tomaka, J., and Kelsey, R. M. (1991). The presence of human friends and pet dogs as moderators of autonomic responses to stress in women. *Journal of Personality and Social Psychology*, 61, pp. 582–589.

Allen, K., Shykoff, B. E., and Izzo, J. L. (2001). Pet ownership, but not ace inhibitory therapy, blunts home blood pressure responses to mental stress, *Hypertension*, 38, 319–324.

Althaus, T. H. (1982). Die Welpenentwicklung beim Siberian Husky. Dissertation Universität Bern. In Feddersen-Petersen, D. (2004). *Hundepsychologie*, 4. Auflage, Stuttgar: Frankh – Kosmos Verlag, p. 237.

Ambros, B. (2012). *Bones of contention: Animals and religion in contemporary Japan*. University of Hawai'i Press.

Anderson, S. (2010). "Animal communication and human language." Prepared for *Cambridge Encyclopedia of the Linguistic Sciences*. Retrieved from http://cowgill.ling.yale.edu/sra/animals_cell.htm. Accessed January 2016.

Arzt, V., Birmelin, I. (1993). *Haben Tiere ein Bewußtsein? Wenn Affen lügen, wenn Katzen denken und Elefanten traurig sind.* [Do pets have an awareness? When apes lie, when cats think and elephants are sad.] München: Bertelsmann.

Ascione, F. R. (1992). Enhancing children's attitudes about the humane treatment of animals: Generalization to human-directed empathy. *Anthrozoös*, 583, pp. 176–191.

Baum, D. (1990). Psychisch kranke Menschen auf dem Pferd. [Mentally ill humans with horses.] In Gäng, M. (Ed.), *Heilpädagogisches Reiten und Voltigieren.* [Curative pedagogy horse riding and vault.] München, Basel: Reinhardt.

Beck, A. M. and Katcher, A. H. (1996). *Between pets and people: The importance of animal companionship* (rev. edition). West Lafayette, IN: Purdue University Press.

Beck, A. M., Katcher, A. H. (1983). *Between pets and people: The importance of animal companionship.* New York: GP Putnam's Sons Pergee Books.

Behaviorist, practice in Germany, in discussion with author, 2016.

Bergesen, F. J. (1989). *The effects of pet faciliated therapy on the self-esteem and socialisation of primary school children.* Paper presented at the 5th International conference on the relationship between humans and animals. Monaco.

Bergland, C., (2015). "Cortisol and oxytocin hardwire fear-based memories." *Psychology Today*, July 10, 2015. Retrieved from www.psychologytoday.com/blog/the-athletes-way/201507/cortisol-and-oxytocin-hardwire-fear-based-memories. Accessed May 2017.

Bergler, R. (1986). *Mensch und Hund Psychologie einer Beziehung*. [Humans and dogs psychology of a relationship.] Köln: edition agrippa GmbH.

Bergler, R. (1995). *Warum Kinder Tiere brauchen*. [Why children need animals.] Freiburg i. Br.: Herder.

Bloch, G. (2004). *Der Wolf im Hundepelz. Hundeerziehung aus unterschiedlichen Perspektiven*. [Wolves in dogs four. Dog training from different perspectives.] Stuttgart: Kosmos Verlag.

Bloch, G., Marriott, J. E. (2016). *The pipestone wolves: The rise and fall of a wolf family*. Calgary: RMB Rocky Mountain Books.

Bloch, G., Radinger, E. (2010). *Woelfisch fuer Hundehalter, von Alpha, Dominanz und anderen populaeren Irrtuemern*. [Wolves-language for dog owners, about alpha, dominance and other misapprehensions.] Stuttgart: Kosmos Verlag.

Boroditsky, L., Schmidt, L. and Phillips, W. (2003). Sex, syntax, and semantics. In Gentner, D. and Goldin-Meadow, S. (Eds.), *Language in mind: Advances in the study of language and cognition*. London: Cambridge University Press, 61–80.

Bryant, B. K., Whorley, P. (1989). *Child-petrelationships under conditions of maternal inavailability*. Paper presented at 5th International conference on the relationship between humans and animals. Monaco.

Bustad, L. K., Hines, L. M. (1983). Placement of animals with the elderly: Benefits and strategies. In Katcher, A. H., and Beck, A. M. (Ed.), *New perspectives on our lives with companion animals*. Philadelphia: University Press.

Centers for Disease Control webpage. Retrieved from http://www.cdc.gov/hrqol/wellbeing.htm#three. Accessed May 24, 2016.

Chandler, C. (2012). *Animal assisted therapy in counseling* (2nd edition). New York: Routledge Taylor & Francis Group.

Corson, S. A., Corson, E. O., and Gwyne P. H. (1977). Pet dogs as nonverbal communication links in hospital psychiatry. *Comprehensive Psychiatry*, 18, pp. 61–72.

Corson, S. A., O'Leary Corson, E. O. (1978). Pets as mediators of therapy. *Curr Psychiatric therapy*, 18, pp. 195–205.

Corson, S. A., O'Leary Corson, E. O. (1980). Pet animals as nonverbal communication mediators in psychotherapy in institutional settings. In Corson, S. A., O'Leary Corson, E. O., Alexander, J. A. (Ed.), *Ethology and nonverbal communication in mental health*. Oxford, New York, Toronto, Sydney, Paris, Frankfurt: Pergamon Press.

d'Andrade, R. G. (1984). Cultural meaning systems. In Shweder, R. and LeVine R. (Eds.), *Culture theory: Essays on mind, self, and emotion*, pp. 88–119. Cambridge, UK: Cambridge University Press.

Del Amo, C. (2003). *Probleme mit dem Hund verstehen und vermeiden*. [How to understand the problems of dogs and to avoid them.] Stuttgart: Ulmer Verlag, pp. 9–19.

De Smet, S. (1992). Die Bedeutung von Haustieren für das seelische Erleben von älteren Menschen. [The significance of pets for the spiritual experience of elderly people.] In Gäng. M. (Ed.), *Mit Tieren leben im Alten- und Pflegeheim*. [To live with animals in retirement homes, nursing homes.] München, Basel: Reinhardt.

Dodge, R., Daly A. P., Huyton J., Sanders Lalage D. (2012). The challenge of defining wellbeing. *The International Journal of Wellbeing*, vol. 2, no. 3, pp. 222–235.

Doheny, K., (August 3, 2012). Pets for depression and health. Retrieved from http://www.webmd.com/depression/features/pets-depression#1. Accessed August 2016.

Donaldson, J. (1996). *The culture clash: A revolutionary new way of understanding the relationship between humans and domestic dogs*. Berkeley, CA: James & Kenneth Publishers.

Doris Day Foundation. The empathy connection: Creating caring communities through the human-animal relationship. Retrieved from http://www.humanesociety.org/assets/pdfs/abuse/empathy-connection.pdf. Accessed February 2017.

Eckert, C. (1992). *Tierhaltung im Heim*. [Animal housing in nursing homes.] In Caritas-Korrespondenz, 60, pp. 15–20.

Euromed Info-Bereiche. Retrieved from http://www.euromedinfo.eu/how-culture-influences-health-beliefs.html/. Accessed February 9, 2017.

Feddersen-Petersen, D. (2008). *Ausdrucksverhalten beim Hund. Mimik und Koerpersprache, Kommunikation und Verstaendigung.* [Mode of Expressions of dogs. Mimic and Body Language, Communication and Understanding.] Stuttgart: Frankh-Kosmos Verlag.

Feddersen-Petersen, D. (2004). *Hundepsychologie: Sozialverhalten und Wesen, Emotionen und Individualitaet.* [Dogs Psychology: Social behavior and Nature, Emotions and Individuality.] Stuttgart: Frankh-Kosmos Verlag. pp. 269–270, 293.

Fehrenberg, C. (1993). *Die Mensch-Tier-Beziehung als therapeutische Hilfe in Humanmedizin und Sozialtherapie.* [The human-animal-relationship as therapeutic help in human medicine and social therapy.] Paper presented at the conference "Between Humans and animals," Berlin.

Fine H. (Ed.), Kruger, K. A. and Serpell, A. (2010). Animal-Assisted Interventions in mental health. In *Handbook on animal-assisted therapy. Theoretical foundations and guidelines for practice.* Third Edition, 33–48, San Diego: Academic Press.

Friedmann, E. Katcher, A. H., Thomas, S. A., Lynch, J. J. and Messent, P. R. (1983). Social interaction and blood pressure: Influence of animal companions. *Journal of Nervous and Mental Disease,* 171, 461–464.

Friedmann, E. (1980). Animal companions and one-year survival of patients after discharge from a coronary care unit, *Public Health Report,* 307 ff.

Friedmann, E. (2000). The animal-human bond: Health and wellness. In Fine, A. H., *Handbook on animal-assisted therapy. Theoretical foundations and guidelines for practice.* San Diego: Academic Press.

Fujimura, C. (2005). *Russia's abandoned children: An intimate understanding.* Westport, CT: Praeger Publications.

Grandin, T., Johnson, C. (2005). *Animals in translation.* New York: Harcourt, Inc.

Gray, P., Young, S. (2011). Human-pet dynamics in cross-cultural perspective. *Anthrozoös.,*vol. 24, issue 1, pp. 17–30.

Gäng, M. (Ed.), (1992). *Mit Tieren leben im Alten- und Pflegeheim.* [Live with animals in retirement homes, nursing homes.] Basel: Reinhardt.

Gäng, M. (Ed.), (1990). *Heilpädagogisches Reiten und Voltigieren.* [Curative pedagogy and vault.] München, Basel: Reinhardt.

Gimlik, S. (1996). *Die wohltuenden Wirkungen von Tieren auf Menschen unter dem speziellen Blickwinkel von Menschen mit Behinderungen.* (Master thesis). [The wellbeing effects animals have for humans especially for humans with disabilities.] Staatsprüfung für das Lehramt an Sonderschulen, Universität Würzburg.

Greiffenhagen, S. and Buck-Werner, O. N. (2007). *Tiere als Therapie: Neue Wege in Erziehung und Heilung.* [Animals as a therapy: New ways in education and healing.] Mührlenbach: Kynos.

Greiffenhagen, S. et al. (2007). *Tiere als Therapie.* [Animals as therapy.] Nerdlen: Kynos Verlag Dr. Dieter Fleig GmbH.

Grimm, D. (2014). *Citizen canine: Our evolving relationship with cats and dogs.* New York: Public Affairs.

Grimm, D. (April 16, 2015). *How dogs stole our hearts.* Retrieved from http:// www. sciencemag.org/news/2015/04/how-dogs-stole-our-hearts. Accessed January 21, 2017.

Grigore, A. and Rusu, A. (2014). Interaction with a therapy dog enhances the effects of social story method in autistic children. In *Society and Animals,* pp. 241–261.

Gutzmann, H. (1991). Tiere als Helfer in der Therapie? Argumente für "pet facilitated therapy." [Animals as an assistent in Therapy? Arguments for a pet facilitated therapy."] In Denzin, J. (1991). *Autonomie im Alter.* [Autonomy in the advanced years.] Berlin: Freie Universität.

Gutzmann, H. (Ed.), (1990). *Brennpunkt Gerontopsychiatrie.* [Focus geriatric psychiatry.] Hannover: Vincentz Verlag.

Hahn, Daniela, Geniushof e.V., Esgrus, Schleswig-Holstein, Germany, in discussion with author, January 16, 2017

Hart, L. A. (2010). Positive effects of animals for psychosocially vulnerable people: A turning point for delivery. In A. H. Fine (Ed.), *Handbook on animal-assisted therapy: Theoretical foundations and guidelines for practice*, 3rd Edition, pp. 59–84. San Diego: Academic Press.

Hartwell, I. Annapolis, MD, in discussion with author, February 17, 2017.

Hassink, J., van Dijk, M. (2006). *Farming for health: Green care farming across Europe and the United States of America*. AA Dortrecht Netherlands: Springer Verlag, 315.

Hatch, E. (1973). *Theories of man & culture*. New York and London: Columbia University Press.

Heidegger, M. (2001). *Poetry, language, thought*. New York: Harper Modern Perennial Classics.

Heidemarie, A., Plön, Schleswig-Holstein, Germany, in discussion with author, Feburary 20, 2016.

Hoerster, N. (2004). *Haben Tiere eine Würde? Grundfragen der Tierethik*. [Do pets have a dignity? Basic questions of animal ethic.] München: C. H. Beck.

Hoey, B. (2014). A simple guide to the practice of ethnography and a guide to ethnographic field notes. In *The selected works of Brian Hoey*. Marshall Digital Scholar. Retrieved from http://works.bepress.com/brian_hoey/12. Accessed March 2015.

Hooker, S. D., Freeman, L. H. and Stewart, P. (2002). Pet therapy research: a historical review. *Holist. Nurs Pract.*, October 16, 2002 (5), pp. 17–32. Retrieved from http://www.ncbi.nlm.nih.gov/pubmed/12465214. Accessed November 2016.

Horowitz, A. (2016). *Being a dog: Following the dog into the world of smell*. New York: Scribner.

Hurn, S. (2012). *Humans and other animals: Cross-cultural perspectives on human-animal interactions*, London: Pluto Press.

Igor. Annapolis, MD, in discussion with author, 2016.

J. S. Annapolis, MD, in discussion with author, February 13, 2017.

Jacob, K. (2016). "Helden von Reykjavik." [Heros of Reykjavik.] In *Dogs: Hunde Verstehen und Lieben* [Dogs: Understand and love dogs], pp. 87–93. Accessed March 2016.

Japan Times (2015) Tokyo's menagerie of pet cafes. Accessed January 2017.

Jovasevic, V., Sato, K., Guedea, A. L., Mizukami, H., Nishimori, K., Radulovic, J., Tronson N.C., Guzman, F. (2013). Fear-enhancing effects of septal oxytocin receptors. *Nature Neurosience*, July 21, 2013, vol. 16, pp. p. 1185–1187. Accessed May 2017.

Joy, M. (2010). *Why we love dogs eat pigs and wear cows*, San Francisco: Conari Press.

Kaplan, Helmut F. (1993). *Leichenschmaus. Ethische Gründe für eine vegetarische Ernährung*. [Funeral feast. Ethical reasons for a vegetarian diet.] Hamburg: Rowohlt.

Kaplan, Helmut F. (2003). Die *Ethische Weltformel. Eine Moral für Menschen und Tiere*. [Ethical formula of the world. A moral for humans and animals.] Neukirch-Egnach: Vegi-Verlag.

Kaplan, Helmut F. (2009). *Ich esse meine Freunde nicht oder warum unser Umgang mit Tieren falsch ist*. [I do not eat my friends or why is our contact with animals wrong.] Berlin: Trafo Wissenschaftsverlag.

Katcher, A. H. (1983). Man and the living environment: An excursion into cyclical time. In Katcher, A. H., and Beck, A. M. (Ed.), *New perspectives on our lives with companion animal*. Philadelphia: University Press.

Katcher, A. H., et al. (1983). Looking, talking, and blood pressure: The physiological consequences of interaction with the living environment. In Katcher, A. H., and Beck, A. M. (Ed.), *New perpectives on our lives with companion animals*. Philadelphia: University Press.

Kenway L., Matthew W., (2001). A temporally structured replay of awake hippocampal ensemble activity during rapid eye movement sleep. *Neuron*, no. 1, vol. 29, pp. 145–156.

Kopernick, U. (2013). Pets really do provide health benefits. *New Zealand Health*, January 13, 2013. Retrieved from http://www.nzherald.co.nz/health/news/article.cfm?c_id=204&objectid=10858838. Accessed July 8, 2016.

Kortschal, K. and Ortbauer, B. (2003). Behavioral effects of the presence of a dog in a classroom, *Anthrozoös*, 16, 147–159.

Kortschal, K. (2005). *Why and how vertebrates are social: Physiology meets function.* Plenary contribution given at the International ethological conference, Budapest, Hungary.

Krauss, T. LCDR, Fort Belvior Community Hospital Virginia, Gespraech waehrend eines Vortrages an der USNA. Annapolis, MD, in discussion with author, Feburary 9, 2016.

Kröger, A. (1989). Heilpädagogisches Voltigieren als soziale Aufgabe. [Curative pedagogy and vault as a social duty.] In Kuratorium für Therapeutisches Reiten (Ed.), Heilpädagogisches Voltigieren und Reiten. Das Pferd in Pädagogik, Psychologie und Psychiatrie. [Curative pedagogy, vault and horse riding. Horses in pedagogy, psychology and psychiatric.] *Therapeutisches Reiten.* [Horse riding therapy.] Warendorft: 11ff.

Lampert, M. Annapolis, MD, in discussion with author, February 10, 2017.

Levinson, B. M. (1962). The dog as a co-therapist. *Mental Hygiene*, 46, 59–65.

Levinson, B. M. (1969). *Pet-oriented child psychotherapy.* Springfield, IL: Charles C Thomas.

Levinson.B. (1965). Pet psychotherapy: use of household pets in the treatment of behavior disorder in childhood. *Psychological Reports*, 17, 695–698.

Levinson, B. (1983). The future of research into relationships between people and their animal companions. In Katcher, A. H., and Beck, A. M. (Ed.), *New perspectives on our lives with companion animals.* Philadelphia: University Press.

Lockwood, R. (1983). The influence of animals on social perception. In Katcher, A. H., and Beck, A. M. (Ed.), *New Perspectives on our lives with companion animals.* Philadelphia: University Press.

Lorenz, K. (1978). *Vergleichende Verhaltensforschung. Grundlagen der Ethologie.* [Comparative behavioral. Basic Ethology.] Wien: Springer Verlag.

Lorenz, K. (1995a). *Er redete mit dem Vieh, den Vögeln und den Fischen.* [He talked to cattle, birds and fishes.] München: dtv.

Lorenz. K. (1995b). *So kam der Mensch auf den Hund.* [That is how humans became aware of dogs.] München: dtv.

M., Janina, Glücksburg, Schleswig-Holstein, Germany, in discussion with author, June 2, 2016

M. N., Flensburg, Schleswig-Holstein, Germany, in discussion with author, June 4, 2016

Maeyama-san. Annapolis, MD, in discussion with author, November 12, 2016.

Maeyama Family. Annapolis, MD, in discussion with author, January 4, 2017.

Martin, F., and Farnum, J. (2002). Animal-assisted therapy for children with pervasive developmental disorders. *Western Journal of Nursing Research*, 24, pp. 657–670.

Maslow, Abraham (1954). *Personality and Motivation.* New York: Harper Press.

McComsky und Mugford (1975). Begonien Wellensittich Experiment. [Begonie Budgie experiment.] In Sussman, M. B. (2016). (Ed.), *Pets and the Family.* New York: Routledge.

McConnell, P. B. (2007). *For the love of a dog: Understanding emotion in you and your best friend.* New York: Ballantine Books.

McGrane, S. (July 8, 2013). Moscow's metro dogs. *The New Yorker.* Retrieved from https://www.newyorker.com/culture/culture-desk/moscows-metro-dogs.

Miklosi, A. "The science of friendship." *Scientific American: Special collector's edition.* December 2015.

Millan, C. (2006). *Cesar's Way.* New York: Rivers Press.

Mondry, H. (2015). *Political animals: Representing dogs in modern Russian culture.* Boston: Brill Rodopi.

Moore, R. Annapolis, MD, in discussion with author, December 16, 2016.

Morell, V. (June 9, 2014). *"Love hormone" has same effect on humans and dogs.* Retrieved from http://www.sciencemag.org/news/2014/06/love-hormone-has-same-effect-humans-and-dogs?intcmp=collection-dogs. Accessed January 21, 2017.

Mugford, R. A., and M`Comisky, J. G. (1975). Some recent work on the psychotherapeutic value of cage birds with old people. In Clayton S., and Myers, G. (2015), *Conservation psychology: Understanding and promotion, human care for nature*, p. 25. West-Sussex, UK: John Wiley & Sons Ltd.

"Nature, pleasure, myth animals in the art of Japan." An exhibit at Amherst College. Retrieved from https://www.Amherst.edu/system/files/media/Nature/252C/2520Pleasure/252C/2520Myth_website/2520checklist.pdf. Accessed January 2017.

Nassoufis, A. (December 20, 2012). Haustiere tun ihrem Menschen einfach gut. [Pets comfort a human being's life.] Retrieved from http://www.welt.de/gesundheit/psychologie/article112145958/Haustiere-tun-ihrem-Menschen-einfach-gut.html. Accessed October 20, 2016.

Niepel, G. (1998). *Mein Hund hält mich gesund. Der Hund als Therapeut für Körper und Seele.* [My dog keeps me healthy. Dogs as therapist for Body and Soul.] Augsburg: Weltbild Verlag

Nimer J. and Lundahl, B. (2007). Animal-assisted therapy: A meta-analysis. *Antrozoös*, 20, 225–235.

Niijima, N. (2016). Chats, cats and a cup of tea: a sociological analysis of the neko cafè phenomenon in Japan. In M. Pregowski (Ed.), *Companion animals in everyday life: Situating human-animal engagement within cultures*, pp. 269–282. New York: Palgrave Macmillan.

Odendaal, J. (2000). Animal-assisted therapy—Magic or medicine? *Journal of Psychosomatic Research*, 49, pp. 275–280.

Odendaal, J. and Meintjes, R. (2003). Neurophysiological correlates of affiliative behaviour between humans and dogs. *The Veterinary Journal*, 165, 296–301.

Oertl, M. (1996). Haben Affen doch ein Bewusstsein wie wir Menschen? [Do apes have an awareness like humans do?] *PM Magazine*, 2, 14–21.

Olbrich, E. (1987). *Soziale Unterstützung im Alter: Die Rolle von Mensch und Tier.* [Social support at an old age: Role model of humans and animals.] Universität Erlangen-Nürnberg, Institut für Psychologie. Memorandum No 50.

Olbrich, E. und Otterstedt C. (Ed.), (2003). *Menschen brauchen Tiere, Grundlagen und Praxis der tiergestützten Pädagogik und Therapie.* [Humans need animals, Basics and practice of animal based pedagogy and therapy.] Stuttgart: Franckh -Kosmos Verlags GmbH & Co. KG, 259 ff.

Otterstedt, C. (2001). *Tiere als therapeutischer Begleiter.* [Animals as a therapy companion.] Stuttgart: Franckh Kosmos Verlags GmbH & Co KG.

Pay, R. Annapolis, MD, in discussion with author, March 12, 2015.

Pesmen, D. (2000). *Russia and soul.* New York: Cornell University Press.

Petrzela, Natalia Mehlman (May 1, 2016). "When wellness is a dirty word." In *The Chronicle Review*. Retrieved from http://chronicle.com/article/When-Wellness-Is-a-Dirty-Word/236266. Accessed in May 2, 2016.

Positive Psychology Centre, The University of Pennsylvania. Retrieved from http://ppc.sas.upenn.edu/. Accessed February 20, 2017.

Pregowski, M. P. (2016). *Companion animals in everyday life: Situating human-animal engagement within cultures.* New York: Palgrave MacMillan.

Rogers, C.R. (1973).*Entwicklung der Persönlichkeit. [Development of personality.]* Stuttgart: Klett-Cotta

Rockenbauer, S. (2010). *Tiergestützte Therapie mit Pferden bei Patienten mit emotionaler Instabilität. [Animal based therapy with horses for patients with emotional instability.]* Retrieved from http://othes.univie.ac.at/9529/1/2010-05-04_0401559.pdf (06/2012). Accessed July 28, 2016.

Ross University UK www.veterinary.ross.edu accessed 20. May 2017

Rugaas, T. (2006). *On talking terms with dogs: Calming signals,* Wenatchee WA: Dogwise Publishing.

Rusk H. A., (1972). *A world to care for.* New York: Random House, 68–72.

Ryder, Richard D. (2000). *Animal revolution.* Oxford: Berg/Oxford International Publishers Ltd.

Ryder, R. D. (2011). *Speciesism, painism and happiness. A morality for the twenty-first century.* Exeter: Imprint Academic.

Savishinsky, J. S. (1983). Pet Ideas: The Domestication of animals, human behavior, and human emotions. In Katcher, A. H., and Beck, A. M. (Ed.), *New perspectives on our lives with companion animals.* Philadelphia: University Press.

Scheidhacker, M. (1996). Psychotherapie und Reiten. [Psychotherapy and riding.] In Deutsches Kuratorium für therapeutisches Reiten e.V.*: Zur Arbeit mit dem Pferd in Psychiatrie und*

Psychotherapie. [About the work with a horse in pyschiatry and psychotherapy.] München: S.21ff.

Schöll, C. (2015). *Tiergestützte Pädagogik und Therapie: Betrachtung unter bindungstechnischen Gesichtspunkten.* [Animal based education and therapy: Contemplation of bonding aspects.] Hamburg: Diplomica Verlag GmbH.

Schopenhauer, A. (1963). Aphorismen zur Lebensweisheit. Stuttgart: Reclam. In Kaplan, H. F. (1993). *Leichenschmaus. Ethische Gründe für eine vegetarische Ernährung.* [Funeral feast. Ethical reasons of vegetarian diet.] Hamburg: Rowohlt.

Searle, J. (1965). "What is a speech act?" In Black, M. (ed.), *Philosophy in America.* New York: Cornell University Press, pp. 221–239.

Skabelund, A. H. (2011). *Empire of dogs: Canines, Japan and the marking of the modern imperial world.* Ithaca, NY: Cornell University Press.

Siegel, A. (1962). In Sussman, M. (2016). (Ed.), *Pets and the Family.* New York: Routledge.

Singer, P. (1994). *Praktische Ethik.* [Practically ethic.] Stuttgart: Reclam.

Singer, P. (1996). *Animal liberation. Die Befreiung der Tiere.* [Animal liberation. The release of animals.] Hamburg: Rowohlt.

Singer, P. (2009). *Animal Liberation: The definitive classic of the animal movement.* New York City: Harper Perennial.

Singer, P., Mason, J. (2006). *Eating: What we eat and why it matters.* London: Arrow Books.

Smith, B. (2012). The pet effect: Health related aspects of companion animal ownership. *Australian Family Physician,* vol. 41, no. 5, June, pp. 349–442.

Spaemann, R. (2001). *Grenzen-zur ethischen Dimension des Handelns.* [Limitations of ethical dimension behaviour.] Stuttgart: Klett-Cotta.

Stewart, J. J. (2016). *Vegetarianism and animal ethics in contemporary buddhism.* New York: Routledge.

Swenson, K. (2011). The Bible and human "dominion" over animals: Superiority or responsibility. *Huffington Post.* Retrieved from www.huffingtonpost.com. Accessed May, 2016.

Susan S. J. (2000). Retrieval and reconsolidation: toward a neurobiology of remembering. Learning & Memory, *Neuron,*No.2, Jahrgang 7, 73–84.

Szűcs, E., Geers, R., Jezierski, T., Sossidou, E.N. (2012). Animal welfare in different human cultures: Traditions and religious faiths, *Asian Australasian Journal of Animal Science,* 25(11), 1499–1506. Retrieved from http://www.ncbi.nlm.nih.gov/pmc/articles/PMC4093044/. Accessed February 19, 2016.

Tajer, Carlos (2012). Thinking medicine metaphorically, *Argentine journal of cardiology,* vol. 80, no. 6. 485–493.

Taravikova, Elena, Moscow, filmed by Valentine Abramova July 6, 2014 https://www.youtube.com/watch?v=uwkWKfReisA. Accessed December 2016.

Tellington-Jones, L., and Taylor, S. (1993). *Der neue Weg im Umgang mit Tieren. Die Tellington Touch Methode.* [The new way to interact with animals. Tellington-touch technique.] Stuttgart: Franckh-Kosmos.

Thompson, P. R. et al. (1982). Cross-species analysis of carnivore, primate and hominid behaviour. In Feddersen-Petersen, D. (2004). *Hundepsychologie. Sozialverhalten und Wesen, Emotion und Individualverhalten,* 4. Auflage, Stuttgart: Frankh-Kosmos Verlag, p. 236.

Turner, D. C. Interview July 8, 2012. Retrieved from http://www.welt.de/wissenschaft/umwelt/article108504911/Katze-und-Menschen-sollten-mehr-miteinander-sprechen.html. Accessed March 1, 2017.

University of California. www.vetmed.ucdavis.edu. Accessed May 20, 2017.

University of Knoxville Tennessee. www.catalog.utk.edu. Accessed May 20, 2017.

Uvnas-Moberg, K., and Petersson, M. (2005). Oxytocin a mediator of anti-stress, well-being, social interaction, growth and healing. *Zeitschrift für Psychosomatische Medizin und Psychotherapie* [Magazin of psychosomatic medicine and psychotherapy], 51, pp. 57–80.

Uvnas-Moberg, K., Arn, I., and Magnusson, D. (2005). The psychobiology of emotion: The role of the oxytocinergic system. *International Journal of Behavioral Medicine,* 12, pp. 59–65.

Uvnas-Moberg, K., Björkstrand, E., Hillegaart, V. and Ahlenius, S. (1999). Oxytocin as a possible mediator of SSRI-induced antidepressant effects, *Psychopharmacology.* 142, pp. 95–101.

Uvnas-Moberg, K., Handlin, I., and Petersson, M. (2011). Promises and pitfalls of hormone research in human-animal interaction. In P. McCardle, S., McCune, J. A. Griffith, and Maholmes, V. (Ed.), *How animals affect us: Examining the influences of human-animal interaction on child development and human health*, pp. 53–81, Washington, DC: American Psychological Association.

Vormbrock, J. K., and Grossberg, J. M. (1988). Cardiovascular effects of human-pet dog interactions. *Journal of Behavioral Medicine*, 11, pp. 509–517.

Waldau, Paul (2002). *The specter of speciesism: Buddhist and Christian views of animals.* New York: Oxford University Press.

Walker, E. (2011). A woman's biological need to nurture and how to satisfy it when you are not a mom. *Psychology Today,* March 7, 2011. Accessed December 15, 2015.

Walker, M. P., Stickgold, R., (2004). Sleep-dependent learning and memory consolidation, *Neuron,* vol. 44, no. 1, pp. 121–133.

Weiger, Pasadena, MD, in discussion with author, December 3, 2015.

Wells, M., and Perrine, R. (2001). Critters in the cube farm: Perceived psychological and organizational effects of pets in the workplace. *Journal of Occupational Health Psychology*, 6(1), 81–87. http://dx.doi.org/10.1037/1076-8998.6.1.81.

Wiliams, R. (1983). *Keywords: A vocaburlary of culture and society.* New York: Oxford University Press.

Wierzbicka, A. (1997). *Understanding cultures through their key words: English, Russian, Polish, German, and Japanese.* Oxford: Oxford University Press.

Wohlfahrt, R., Mutschler, B., and Bitzer, E. (2013). Wirkmechanismen tiergestützter therapie. FITT Forschungsbericht, April 2013, p. 8. Retrieved from http://tiere-begleiten-leben.de/fileadmin/medien/tiere-begleiten-leben/Forschung/Forschungsbericht_4_Wirkmechanismend_Tgt.pdf. Accessed September 2015.

Wohlleben, Peter (2016). *Das Seelenleben der Tiere: Liebe, Trauer, Mitgefuehl-erstaunliche Einblicke in eine verborgene Welt.* [The life of animals' soul: love, mourning, empathy-amazing insights into a hidden world.] Munich: Verlagsgruppe Random-House.

Wolf, Ursula (Ed.) (2008). *Texte zur Tierethik.* [Articles of animal ethic.] Stuttgart: Reclam Verlag.

Zamir, T. (2006). The moral basis of animal-assisted therapy. *Society & Animals*, vol. 14, no. 2, pp. 179–198.

Zulkifli, I. (2013). Review of human-animal interactions and their impact on animal productivity and welfare. *Journal of Animal Science and Biotechnology*, July 15, 2013. Retrieved from https://jasbsci.biomedcentral.com/articles/10.1186/2049-1891-4-25. Accessed August 2016.

Index

aggression: of Alzheimer's patients, 14; child animal abuse and adult, 55; classroom dogs decreasing student, 15, 55; dog socialization and, 58, 65; human emotions and dog responses of, 77–78; human greeting rituals and dog responses of, 76; human misinterpretation of dog, 47, 51; mother to puppy behavior transfers, 69; playful energy leading to, 78; team work training for, 70

agility training, 26, 37, 65

Ahisma, 28

aigan dobutstu, 30

Air Force Convalescent Hospital, 3

Alzheimer's disease, 14

anger, xiii, 17

animal abuse: animal therapy as, 88–89; by children, studies on, 55; dog neglect, 50; owner-pet model as animal victimization, 27, 28, 43

Animal Assisted Therapy (AAT): animal selection for, 8; benefits and effectiveness of, 16–18; definition, 7; equine, 11–12; history of, 1–7; human-animal teams, relationship descriptions, 19; literature and scholarly studies on, xviii; moral implications of, 88; professional unification needs in, 7; species selection for, 8, 18; training requirements, 7, 10, 17. *See also*

therapy dogs

animal care, 12, 13, 17, 61, 88

animal ethics: animal therapy and issues of, 88–89; farm industry and, 66, 67; Japanese lifestyles and pet ownership, 32; overview and development of, 66–67; veterinary care decisions, 63–64

animal ownership: animal social status, 19, 27, 34–35, 43; animal victimization, 27, 28, 43; as dominion, 25, 27, 28, 43; pets as humans, 27, 42–43, 44–45, 46–48, 67; pets as property, xxi, 25, 30, 42, 43, 44; pets versus livestock, perception comparisons, 66; therapeutic benefits dependent on past, 17–18

animal protection, 18–20, 33–34, 79, 88

animals, overview: cultural views and treatment of, 23–24; dominion over, 23, 25–26, 27–28; emotions of, 19–20; human-animal relationship benefits, 88; religious traditions on, 24, 27–28; sleep cycles of, 79–80; social status of, 19; well-being of (positive human contact), 63–66. *See also specific species*

animal sacrifice, 33

Animals Help People (club), 6

Animals in the Art of Japan (exhibition), 29

animal therapy (animals-as-healers), overview: cultural influences on beliefs of, xiv; history of, 1–7; literature and

99

About the Authors

Clementine Fujimura is a cultural anthropologist (PhD 1993, the University of Chicago) who has conducted research and published on the subjects of youth welfare and marginalization in Russia and the United States as well as on military culture. A professor at the United States Naval Academy, Dr. Fujimura teaches on the subjects of intercultural communication, cultural anthropology, as well as Russian and German languages and cultures. In her spare time, Dr. Fujimura trains in search and rescue with her Belgian Malinois, Scipio, and as a volunteer for Hospice of the Chesapeake and military communities with her therapy certified dachshund, Rosie.

Simone Nommensen is a veterinarian from the LMU University in Munich, Germany. Since 2002 she has also worked as an animal behaviourist in her practice in Schleswig Holstein. Beyond her clinical and behavioral work, she is passionately involved in search and rescue with her Vizsla, Neo, and as a licensed trainer of dogs. In her spare time, Nommensen lectures and conducts workshops on animal communication and behavior.